A Sing Economy——published by **flim forum press**——po box 549, slingerlands, ny, 12159——www.flimforum.com——**flim forum press** is + *A Sing Economy* edited by: matthew klane + adam golaski——films: scott puccio——printed by: boyd printing co., albany, ny——ISBN 978-0-9790888-1-0——*A Sing Economy* copyright——© 2008 by: **flim forum press**, all rights reserved, poems copyright © by our authors——**flim forum press**——

A Sing Economy

from How We Saved the City

Kate Schapira

Magical Urbanism

I was walking home when a glow caught my eye: the mulch around a municipal tree was burning. Got down to scrape it out and found there was more than I thought. A couple of men walking the other direction saw and stopped to help me, using a corner of loose brick. They were black, and I spared a thought for how I could have reacted while we were squatted down getting the last embers: we dusted our hands off, a line in my head captured the little glows. *The evening was alive with first responders*, already turning it, and then our respective cities closed over us again.

Safe as Houses

To belong to ownership: a twist too neat for inverse. The signs are going up
everywhere, like rabbits along the highway. Looking around, we see them. Root
the birds' -nest fungi out of the aloe pot. Humble underpinnings, that desire has.
Safe to own: the warp in your board, meld in your corner, to set your windows
in. We should hang out our shingle: one kind of math or another done here. Every
tenant's shingle should be out. The floor slopes from its hump. Time paid for by
the wet trees that surround us explains the difference between "fewer" and "less."
Properties. And less. Ownership links and sets through the city, puts on, shrugs off.
Shuns and shuts out the bleared opposite.

Architecture supports each moment financially, moments that could be floating
their independence over bridges. So say borrowed dwellers, tender more (weirdly,
mathematically) to some moments than others. Not dream-logic but of the dream
house, it proceeds, we can state about it. A waterdrop changes the shapes of
everything nearby through reflection, not accuracy, just reflection. It isn't a true
mirror or a rear-view or a mugger's mirror or the one James found on garbage
night, big as me, with carven frame. All over the city in the waterdrop members of
a privileged group rise early and snap at their husbands.

The belief that ownership will save the city qualifies, comes under the heading,
or falls. It's like saying that slow dreamlike boats piloted by mimes will, or dirty
Valkyries on bikes. It's like going without saying to a city made of wood, PVC pipe
and brick, bundles of hair that used to be rats and tax forms and windows that can't
be saved, this way: teetering on the lip of preservation. Sill of surface tension. City
snapped at that moment. The key on rent day sears the hand, the office cools me
by name, I hand over my math. Posters up for the New Urbanism, olive- and rust-
colored friendly fire. Blades of fans that fall with a crash for no reason, or a rented
wind. Apartment like paid silence; house, an alibi. Fewer lots, but less time.

Weird Math I

+ dishes by hand – no dishpan, inefficient + organic lettuce and carrots + she smiles at me – down the disposal – outside my neighborhood (– I make my paper copies – their chemicals) + health-food dish soap – in the brick zombies of my friends' old home (– driving to get them – don't know who picked them – for the chain store – trucked them) – lights on in the kitchen – on North Main Street – at Eagle Square – (the honor system + lingering) – in plaza geometry – good edible particles – uncertain goya and eggplant + dishwasher we don't use – driving distances – filling with swampy runoff – mosquito larva – bleaching it =

The curve, also, of responsible eating; the heart of heat, a swab of feeling guilty,
cold against rigor in accounting laying the curve over; refuge in columns. That
one could neutralize or cancel the other out. Math takes many forms: installment
plans, first last and security, name earrings, art in the blood, dogs, speculative
development, the dimensions of banners, two or three to a bed, accounts, changes
of dressing per day, acreage, penny-pinching, reciprocal favors, head counts, square
screen inches.

Which was made. Which just grew. A cloud falls on thinking, a math that
precipitates, crystallizes into the purity of inaction above the branded smokestack,
the factory air, stiller and stiller until the snow comes. If sorry doesn't count,
guilt is not disinfectant, just cold. Those old calipers from our measuring days,
ourselves as engines, parts, the mills to work lace, humming looms, the looming
floss. Architecture is chambered for comparison, releases to the operation each
component, each human bead and wire responsible for its own turning.

The distributive. Property. Guilt is weird math because it attempts to resolve, it
obscures the heart till I can't think where it's gone. The same to both sides as if
I hadn't done anything, as if balancing. Separates. Cities superscripted, motions
between them rimmed in glass. Opening between them like the mouths of birds.
Like the difference between mouths of birds and their nests.

Weird Math II

The beauty of marble over the beauty of succession. It is always as if heavy plunder were being spoken. Humans manacle each other to the lives they have, end to end. *The constraints of their former positions have unfortunately not allowed them the time to engage in the larger neighborhood.*

In a city of elimination it became necessary to bulldoze in order to save. Save on chips. Save on shoes. Save on a thirty-six-inch flat-screen, on leather couches, on bedroom sets, a short amount each month, each month longer and longer, a beautiful chainsaw of profit. To fill the house with blossoming sound. *It is certainly possible to grow an environment.*

Snapping at moments, answering questions they brought, *they came here with a respect for historic preservation and all the work that has been done to rehabilitate old structures.* Of shining stones, exclusive shining. A free publication in the bank lobby. The luxury issue.

The ghost story says they came here to better themselves. To have things. To do. Their kids to get part-time jobs, then to look fully good. The money the family thinks: there's money and then there's money that's far away. *In the end, they feel that it has simply discredited their name.*

Construction equates hope with speculation. With the overcast, *the existing community offers a rich fabric* up as a sacrifice. Offers coexistence up. Unzips the skyline upward, the city suit, casts it, sure that one succeeds the other. You don't grow an environment, it grows you. The math of apparitions states: if it appears, it is.

In an equation, I feel for them. In an inequality, I can't. As real as you can't see, examination hews closer first. To home. The city. The city's people. The armaments of luxury.

The letters, the levels, the vagueness, the wait. Everything set up to trap every day. Neither the *santos* nor the local product even make a dent in the prospect of remarkable living, *the ability to displace long-standing residents and bring about.* Everyone will still have to be somewhere, the dust of construction like pollen.

If anything is justifiable then anything is. Therefore a basic city of thinking changes hands, no changes, but thinking again. That the right choice rolls out a wide flat path that says do this *forgive me* because *because* applied to the future becomes the dangerous *therefore*. From cause to cry the danger birds' high spiral. One chases off another but it's not the one you think until they are too high to see. After which the city you've made dives in and out of the one you think, cormorant in a dirty river.

Absolute integer of your acts *and what else* buzzing up there like thousands of ships or ghosts of flies. Assurances around the spires sharpened for a reason. If you believe equivalency you'll believe the fruits of it. Action as amulet, chains you vote for, leaf through the ledger of previous choices you believe is chained to you, recorded from the pocket all your deeds your leases your ownership extended to you as long as the fall birds shall incontinently happen. Name the storms that blow them to protect yourself.

Paper is wonderful ink is wonderful facts are recognizable facts are familiar paper is familiar the same barrier. Lesser evil shudders into a lower order when you think. Would you rather see the city roll down this side or that of the *thankless task*, the hill. Work to see uppermost in succession. Or at once see. That which is not sound in the timber is not sound in the fall.

Justification rolls over making over injury injuring everyone with need. Scrutiny crumbles its own so far *no* further the horns of wind blowing at dawn through *no* an alarm. Have I kept the public domain waiting in the morning tangled room waking panic, justification peeling in, do you deserve to have your motes free in the air. Can you explain the answers math does not admit.

Can salvation nest into the details can it be plucked like any devil from the burned house *be combed for it* from sanctuary *show me* point your pins into the roots of the nerves where it lives writing this, you too, attempting. No outer garment no other ledger-keeper. Because where do you go from relief that cancellation policy.

Revolving fund

…as a name in concrete is to memory as…
fingertip is to silence…recent
clandestine…where the record of changes is not
in common use…*I have never felt it more*…Newcomers
may well…prised, even remembering they've never
seen what…before. To ensure that…*safe and comfortable*
and to maintain…my all…and successfully. *Enter*
three pieces; give them five ends; hedge out;
…Countenanced. Is my face…All behind us; behind *creative*
People who enrich…but worth their corner.
For wh…noticeable we…mercy in the form
of color, of shoring up,

…of scraping to be done will
…ment, flush or suffusion of this
neighb…it needs: *Put in your goods, keep*
them well handled,

in swirls…*this seemingly class-conscious*…to be
mitred, praised, culturally…inhabited…longer…follows

…*conflict that has apparently*…trying to emulate
minutes of this meeting…bett…keep details
important. As…uable as real
gives out its color in a similar manner. Primary,
a particul…*little idea*…of dream, promontory
from which however little else is visible…

A sign propped on a piece of dry rot and two overturned
buckets: PLEASE USE SIDE ENTRANCE and two
men lean over it, smoking also,…direction…uplift…feeling,
showplace, to be shown, to show places…*I came*
with a respect…brewing…

While…just getting on with it, two women smoke
together and tap on the steps. Look coolly. It's on…side,
on either…of them, the ratty siding…scrapes…
make an echo. Genie Lift in the back yard

shines and contracts to make for you…rection
of any protocol…up, upward, up and coming, unthinking
associations by use of *a sufficient quantity of purple*
archil…*piece of green copperas the size*…*one ounce of*
bluestone of vitriol…Liquescence…asset,
acidulate, the names of chemicals change…and expiration
date for each revo…of doorknob or hinge…where change
comes in,…*more dismissive than cruel*. Pour
and stir motives into the sur…fix…circus colors, service
leak, bought up and stained…rfeit as we can imagine. Mordants…

dyes last,…tangible…the change
readily imparted by the following simple process,…how
much better motives are under…how much we've…*It will*
be understood how…an aim…or not the houses empty, voices
heard…*It is with much regret that I have lost*…

older undercoat…flat, as if choral,
but shallowly. *This finishes them*. …questionably
…a position to question. …*a fine gloss*.

This vat continues to be
good until exhausted, hence "revolving" for whi…
used also…guards set over new
cement in folding chairs to prevent a few
blocks away where names bites into the bottom of lampp…

to make people feel safe…paint…*no*
confidence…a show of feeling…*a rich fabric*…

Interdependence Day

James and I walk to the Bell Street Park, where we were married. The cool fragrant evening a switch of my vision makes magical: yellow lights softening, dandelion heads, looking up under the conifers at James' suggestion. "That's where I saw the hawk couple having their snack." It's not because I'm personally content: I'm anxious, I'm bleeding, my mouth tastes like old coffee, I'm worried about my sister, I have to pee… Nothing is unmarred, nothing is the way we already imagined it. Because of this, we have to imagine what has never been, can speak about it with hope instead of certainty.

from **Bartimus** / *from* **pony pills**

Barrett Gordon

The world bunks with gods

I WAS IN THE THICK
of it   had a mask at the
back of my head to
keep the beasts starved
my flesh still poison
i wanted to learn a new
fact about the body I
could not control

got   felt
stalking   by 2 flutter-
crippled   eyes   this

summer   while the radio
pirate anchored up to a
satellite in the can-am
border   no-man's-land
the blue flag   she   cuts
down the niagara

i think to myself god-
damn like a man awoke

our last palindromic yr.
this life we had 2! -who
gives, but- bartimus
does not know when
this train began moving,
palindromically   mistook
the other trains for our
departure   thinks
someone has replaced a
very small decoration in
the   room   with
something the same size
just barely a different
color

i've   entertained   the
syndicate fear

why are most the leaves
s p o t t e d   this year
and before they   drop?
why is the dalmatian the
mascot of our paper?

---

inertia of this report   spotted
in   a   weight   of   words'
arrest on st. jersey st.

mirrors are the film

INVENTIVE LOGIC IN PLACE OF THIS SELF-
defeat and scientific whip!   who does all
this thinking?!   this is like the big people
ranking themselves against the little
wearing the little people's clothes / who
were you with before all this / I'm hanging
out / this is mirror talk?   so many models
before us, lean into the sun / so much to go
against   strata   trying
(impossible?) wanting to go back / enough
so ideas   fruit   perhaps
investigate an impossible   consider
planting -yesterday's impossible   tomorrow
unlikely   we see more and *less* now than
ever before   is that a binary rule? do we
need to take a very literal excursion?
beginning to think yes   strip back this sunny
shlak   where are my tears!   is there time for
the world after us   to save this place pretty
soon   who crave this shell /   shave this
hellbeard by june

the trash compounds / mowed into the
molten street high noon / it's pretty– / city
seashells / weed sells / & fem bombshells
/ down by the lake shore

the likes

IT DWARFED ME   MADE A TROLL
tinier   her insatiable chip   like
how quick the flies find you when
you're dead   as if there was never
love between you
it's the irony   my city living
against her quick country pace   my
pulse   good   slow
allow   the   languorous
happenstancial immersion suitable
to speak in ink w/ you   who plants
me in the eye   as we pass each
other in the streets all day

sensory-inflected

AFTER THE SHOW ALVIN F. SPOKE
on elvin j.   how he wasn't going 1
and 2 and dotted quarter notes and
all that in his head   but   pang and
pang /pang pa   pang   rhythm gone
from   ever   meddled   infantry of
positive   space
rather   negotiating it   out there in
the bound
give
bound
give

inclusive   negative   unbe-
queathable   music   of   hingespilt
wings   informed   /then
now/   —that   universal   lingua
franca*ly*   resides   in   ways   **not**
beyond   us   —shame, the   simpli-
cities   we   crush   with   our   sign-
carrying elephant tongues   ever
counting on   building out

value   outlasts   money   american-
ized human   writ   in   to his   story
alienated   rendered   homeless by
its   coxswain   simultaneously
ensnailed   in   its   spiraling
headquarter   spirit   politicked   by
the god-awful which compels it to
the grounds—for   birthmarks to be
                            rubbed back

Question is,
you're who?

TREES OUTSIDE THE DEAF
school sag with winter fruit
I saw them sewing more snow-
shrubs   cycling the roads
before expected comes
the voice
a spool of scarf
off boxwood bush
on   the santa-western coast
         now   hazarding to say
         loves the column in the
new rag   the perpetually
undecorated post
of 'bardamous' as the cafe-
teria casheer   respellt it
         realize   this could
change things in the blinking
         world   could
change chimes
         another   note now
a native belle   maybe calls-
   earth-sugar   some-
thing behind

                 apush
                 helping

  record opens   the can
of words but   works
as only   patches can

dreams   reels   other
paraphernalia of transit   this
is the train   this   charge
above the   train

a 3rd

it never began
which was the thing
being itself
why would it all
it had doing was the slipping
in & out of socks nothing
but the squelch
of the makeshift
galosh   how
a bird would land it
nip the words
admittedly black, wirey like crisp ant
but planed as Modigliani eyes
it never began
was always
could be pet
just not rubbed
not danced most
likely not oiled
just fracted
bled &
swum out
this wasn't it
avoiding work which, it
wasn't above
the instrument was, above.
the 2-D's 'elongated' at
the 'taking up'
this *not* moving
& it took 2 to 3
possible non-names on
          & this is how
it rose from grace

something's snowing april
down her back-to-baby jowl
not yet roost parts loosen
from the feet i think
float some pigeon snow
who doesn't land trees this
year's notice i'd learned to
swallow five pony pills at
once w/ water
thinking about the dog w/ the bird
st. pat's river back to
green of algae
restorative declines
dust caked top the crowsfeet
sumac trees top/trump dead-
rooves just clouds sud barely weighted
bus sides say light rain
showing dancers
a new musical i wonder

the sunning forms
are unshaped from
blather specifically
the unconsequenced
face having
received my words
the value of speech reappears mom-
entarily to be trampled by the eyes moving
into unfit breasts
sharing the echo of foot's step
smalls of backs to rumps
noting impact too in
the stores at
leg's roof
my voice too low
anyhow to pool
the bowls about their ears
the hair tucked behind them
unapproved, worrisome, ok
but the photographer's craft is compromised
by the gaze
horizon chops their
 heads off in the composition
even the older gal looking on runs
down their beachballs on wind
blushing
& in the shade
the thoughts cool not

hi ella there's
coffee water
sun back in the
ears red with
nape & wrists
behind / below
all red
all red
at room temp
& rolés mops it from
the butcher's
floor, ridgeland
tho it runs beneath as
you both wells know

uninconvenienced by
your busy silence—i'm sure
—you're marrying eachother
i'll just show up
"i" did in duke's dream
running to the party
sculptable
nice country road buzz
everyone married
i pinch me
still zigging across NY
state hitting weddings rabbits
somewhat spaced out beer wells
& then b/c i was "violently" sailing
over a fence
as he put it, the new
throng alarmed from
"his" building
would point
at me
the fickle dream morphs
a giant rakes up
the friend (me) man-
handles him like the butter-
fly left with baby
i'm listening, barb
nicked me is all
mary pointed out that's
flirting & i'm cross the
ass was that winked
i'm in love at
home in the world
this hallway where i work'll
pan to anything that moves &
love would
not have been invented
here but
outside where
one altogether Glances

aaaaaaaaaaaaaalice

Jennifer Karmin

UNDERNEATH

even if my head would go through

rain for rent

the liquor store
has milk
for $1.99
extra large eggs
for 99 cents

enjoy the sport
of country club
living

freeway entrance
vs. thruway
or expressway

your shoes are
weird

that store sells
donuts and chinese food

self serve
church of christ
meets here

cattle for sale

**it would be
of very little use
without
my shoulders**

we've reached

the point

where

we understand

we've reached

the

point where

we understand a little

we've reached the

point where we

understand

a little

these days

it used to be

difficult

but we've

reached the

point where we

understand a little these days

at the beginning
it was difficult
but we've reached
the point where we
understand a little
these days

yes but i grow at a reasonable pace

ok
rub your
thumb and index
finger together

not sure
shrug your
shoulders

good luck
keep your
fingers crossed

be quiet
put your
finger on your
lips

to be angry
poke your
finger

you may
also try
to beckon
just a moment
thumbs up
thumbs down

**not
in that
ridiculous fashion**

it's

never high

it's not very

high

it's not a

bit high

it's

not at all

high

it's not

especially high

it's

really not high

it's ordinarily not

high

it's
not
so
high
we'll
probably
be amazed

you might

sandwiches
taste better
when they are
cut diagonally
feed the
mayonnaise
to the tuna
               knock
it's april
now it's april
again
the dog still
looks up   **and**

in a dream
dad says
you are dead too

woulda
coulda
shoulda   **i**

no
moe doesn't say
ouch
                     could
let
you
out

instead of

nails

we used

screws

instead

of milk

we

used water

instead of hot

water

we used

cold water

instead of gas we

used electricity

instead
of nothing
we had
everything

THRUWAY

then

keep your feet
moving

buy apple juice

you   stand outside
what it feels like
to not be

on a bus

wonder where
all the roads
go

when your period
will come again

watch a man
walk his
dog

should   say hello
to the girl
who says
hello
to everybody

what's your name
she asks the old man
with cowboy boots
red baseball cap
going to reno

my name's peter
like peter rabbit

say what you mean

it's different

depending on the

year
it's

different depending

on the day

it's different

depending

on the time

it's different

depending

on the

place
it's different depending

on the person

it's different

depending

on

the thing

it's different depending on the

weather

it's different depending

on it's different

it's
different
depending
on
us

i'm not particular as to size

feet smell
noses run
writing as
a way of
life

you lose head
from your heat

you lose heat
from your head

wake up
can't find shoes
or notebook

greenriver is
the watermelon
capital of the world

to look different
to have a
bigger smile

only one
doesn't like
changing
so often
you know

we

waited until

the car

got old

we waited

until

the movie began

we

waited until the ship

went out

we waited until a

friend came

we waited
until
everyone
stood up

everyone has won

children playing
drive with
care

have exact
fare ready

escalator
out of use

please
deposit
litter in
baskets

beware
bags look
alike

all seats
bookable
in advance

we regret
any inconvenience

**and
all must
have prizes**

a

round one

or

square one

a thin

one

or thick

one

a low one

or

high one

a dark one or

light one

this one

or

that one

8 *from* **Huracan's Harp**
electrical disturbances propagate . . .
Survey

Stephanie Strickland

42

the same interaction the same charge and enormous

speed my brother Finn my virtual my transient

twin seething with energy some

or none or any at all

except that one

number that makes me

real and not

him he the ghostly the free

loader the thief exuberant slid in under the bell

electrical disturbances propagate through space as

waves

                making the stream move back and   forth as it moves
                  &
        up
                down

                        circling

                                in

                        space

                streaming

space

                moving at thespeed light light
                                  light dr
                                  light   ifts
                                    light

                                            drifts

                                                            light

                        is

        what

                cannotbe

                                        hurried . . . hurriedcannot
                                        behurried

122

great Pan is dead
the projection withdrawn damp
leatherclad greenmen melt into the woods

       (idolizing idle incubus's
incubation idyll isolated
        individual infatuates itself)

strongboxable the hoaxable
soul of Samson hacked
metaphorms

8

from hush to hosanna the voice-
tweaking knife
technology music sacrifice—

        reborn every *doubling* or *halving*
        of length of string the trouble of 2 to be
        barren the *same* every doubling or—

gap
already called evil non-fit the octave refuses (inside
of which all tone comes to birth)

        subordinate cycles a fifth or a third do not
        evenly fit
        Ṛg Vedic man defined via hymns

numbers (tunings) alive with disagreement
leftover intervals *within* tetrachords
third caste semi-tones

        micro-intervals fourth caste commas
        subliminal
        to the ear in melodic context

audible in monochords—gap
bit
between the real we need and the nearest rational

                                via smallest primes
                                resonance
                                hybrid e.g. benzene alternating between

ring structures neither of which *sigh* really
exists
none of the catastrophes are separate as they happen

                                supernova debris
                                bullet-crazed glass
                                fold on the point of closing

a particular X-tream between Q and A
a specific cognitive disso dance
9 rasas 9 muses 9 grams 9 emotions

on that brink
the waveform alphabets spell states of mind perhaps
perhaps by neural extraction

Ibrahim Adil Shah II renowned for having sought
between Shiyas and Sunnis between Hindus and Muslims
harmony through music

founded a township Navraspur to give shape to his idea of a musical city
in the 17th century speaking
fluently Kannada Marathi Dakhani Urdu

the Bijapur MP and former Union Minister said
the Adil Shahi monuments through lying in neglect have heritage value
tourism potential

he demanded completion of a broad gauge line at once
commissioning an airport
he has taken up the issue with the BJP party leadership

he said I will not participate till Bijapur district gets a Cabinet berth
he said I am boycotting the function on the Gol Gumbaz premises
the musical city

sublime zimzum Persephone contracted Peirce pure zero
Lucretian swerves plummet Peirce purse zero
Valentinian gnosis woad clove Peirce poor zero

failed Puritan American so infinitely kind
to your unmarried wife tinkerer mensch αlpha Indus ωmega
hoofwork script thirdness diagram numbers

and you nether Ereshkigal mimophonic
every dawn every dusk pour me out on the sand
sluice my letters from the slate

without knowledge to obtain the effects of knowledge
    carpenter bee
    cervical ganglia

heaped up wave hanging in the air for centuries
    key conservation
    (not a hair lost)

effected inside glial cells not volumes what is
    storied
    in volumes or in acid-free bits is

on (the) line constantly conversing with the blowing sheet
    impeding
    the bee

rupture is complete with the CD
photons abrade no mass
unlike the scragnail stylus scraping the groove
emancipation of memory from touch has been fulfilled

capture complete whatever the sun *looks* like it's doing
it's not only old witches or wives
connect by look man-shaped mandrake root deep
connection is unseen by (unseen) rules

protocols seeds only some evolve a feel
(that wizard René Thom) for how rules live or for what
lives in them as emergent as appearing after all
tightly seamed to seeming ground ground

ruling in its rolling *is* best of breed code executing
while light show crowds exchange shot | shot | shot dream

170

Subject: [webartery] Short Graphism
From: "Alan Sondheim" <sondheim@panix.com>
Date: Fri, June 9, 2006 2:58 am

To: webartery@yahoogroups.com
Priority: Normal

Infinitely thin projective slice
of difficult equation. The compression

comes to grip[s] with it. There may
be shadows of the future, I don't

know . . . coordinates are
always variable. When the space

moves, the[y] become ill.
Don't they?

Elsewhere,
the real renders. Here it has already given up.

http://www.asondheim.org/graph10.mov
http://www.asondheim.org/graph20.mov

Survey

rubble Deep Field every quarter square degree
of sky a moonsworth : probing (counting mirroring …)
"discovers"

All   iron anywhere aluminum vanadium Orange trees

in the universe   Matter less
than one tenth-of-one
per

/   cent

… Dominance of dark : Sloan survey at Sunspot
rogue infernos coiled wheels making up
time   the starry SFX

dominantly

dark :
so it is written   faint
hiss of tumblers as the safe cracks

rare and *threatened*

numbed by prevalence   quintillions   *bio-*
devour   not a bomb
a hailed brother

over

whelmed
thin
dime

from **The New Poetics**

Mathew Timmons

The New Acrostic

From philosophy comes The New Acrostic (a fashion going back to Napoleon), in which the message is given by the initial letters of the precious pendant. Just as the first acrostic marked the stylistic change from the narrative Prologue to the more poetical Preamble, The New Acrostic occurs at a transition and I was just figuring out what TULIP stood for (I'm new to Calvinism too). I appreciate your book and DVD reviews, the inner letters of which are hidden and follow one another in their proper sequence from one visible end to the other visible end of The New Acrostic. Whoever wins the game, in my opinion, will become the next Game Master and set The New Acrostic word. An example of such poetry as required.

The New Caesura

I consider this proclivity on Nietzsche's part to claim himself as The New Caesura of time and history to display a complete lack of sobriety and His belief that he had become The New Caesura, the destiny, and the great divide of history can be ascribed to his "jealousy of Jesus." (Nietzsche, For what it's worth, The New Caesura looks exactly right to me.) Thanks dude, are you coming to the show in Vermont? (I didn't understand the previous symbol for caesura; I have certainly, Finally understood, I believe, that some people are still waiting for The New Caesura. Sorry for the delay, I will submit to it soon.) So, you like The New Caesura? Shit, it's so Damn Amazing. But to some, The New Caesura is just alright, just another version of the old connect — i — cut.

for Harold Abramowitz

The New Concrete Poem
… Related words: Concrete.

Finally The New Concrete Poem, with stretched word, pounded and swooned and reshaped lines.

Splattered with color and colored like a coloring book, extended.

Finally The New Concrete Poem, with stretched word, pounded and swooned and reshaped lines.

The New Egret

The development of The New Egret took place in a field in early 2002. A 22 million dollar contract was awarded to Technip-Coflexip for research and development. The minimum build requirements of The New Egret included 4000 sq ft of air, using one of the preferred builders from earth: Palmira Member No. 241. The expected fluxes in the first Z-burst model were chosen for optimal parameters together with limits for free fluxes in The New Egret limit.

Our numbers indicate an estimate of the cosmic ray data, as in figure 1, whereas The New Egret flux is shown only as an external function, as an option within The New Package—as an option within The New Egret package. We've also made use of The New Egret to generate data published since our last paper. Our analysis now indicates that the massive black hole we hypothesized will probably not come from an infraction of The New Egret. The numbers indicate only a fraction of The New Egret. More significantly, when comparing The New Egret to the inner Galaxy above, the spectrum is much too difficult.

The shape of the curve between redshifts is mainly determined by the evolution index.

Our members have identified The New Egret as Phase-Averaged Emission derived from the photon spectrum. The numbers only indicate a fraction of The New Egret, an estimate of the extragalactic diffusion. As seen from Fig. 9, The New Egret position is well within the error box and is consistent with its position. In this manner, The New Egret hinders the photonflux in a severely limited region and has contributed to the decay of X-particles.

Also, note The New Egret just across the river. We are tracking activity at thirty nests, and have used the data to form The New Egret.

The New Egret strongly disfavours extragalactic boundaries, thus top-down fluxes limit the various upper neutrinos instead of The New Egret limit. Here, The New Egret limit is lower than the set of errors easiest to see in the maps of The New Egret. In several energy ranges, the high-resolution figures are grouped together with various limits of neutrino fluxes—also note The New Egret limit.

With The New Egret as a Trailblazer we made a logo for T-shirts as supplies allowed. The New Egret, of course beautifully complements the Ibis and Osprey, and is designed to ensure they flow together seamlessly.

An abstract catalog on 'grazars' (blazers which are observed to be high-energy gamma-ray sources), has brought together gamma-ray emissions from directions that are modulated by the Cen X-3 pulsar spin period, all leading us to identify The New Egret as the source. The New Egret observations have not yet been successfully exploited to discriminate among the various proposed models without violating The New Egret bounds.

Similiar to the case of the Z burst model, The New Egret will be The New Emotion (p77) once it is given to us as one. Windows for Windows.

Many of the bounds derived here were found using The New Egret which allowed us to look at higher energy G rays, furthermore, our analysis of Groups and the community of airplanes, boats and cars, has encountered two problems. Extrapolating from what we've been told about The New Egret we're able to come to two conflicting conclusions 1. It Sucks and 2. Compared to say, Astro City, The New Egret is Sweet.

The angle of The New Egret monitor is odd and getting all ready for the sway of this weird, sweet boat. By the way, if we could afford another boat, we'd buy this one in a second, especially for the way it overlooks the fair 9th course of The New Egret.

The New Egret is a tsunami along with The New Tsuba we ordered from Bugei. We could not get the tsuba to fit back perfect so we had to shave the menugi bamboo neutrinos. If you're in NC and take a tour of The New Egret facility, afterwards you might be tempted to say the perfectly apt phrase, "Hint hint."

for Vanessa Place

The New Emotion

The New Emotion is a collection of Movement: Automatic Mechanical Self Winding Movement. The Key Concept of The New Emotion is a multimodal presentation by a lifelike agent of emotion expression. The computing industry of the 1990s enabled significantly higher image quality, boosting diagnostic accuracy with less radiation exposure giving us The New Emotion. Both formats were sanctioned by the child-rearing theories of the day in which the father was admired for displaying The New Emotion while still remaining a function of The New Emotion.

Medee and The New Emotion he feels towards Creuse—an emotion which he senses is imposed on him by fate—generates his weakness and indecision leading him into The New Emotion, turning the tables on Satisfaction and toning his arms for Smartness. Tables possess all of The New Emotion, turning the tables by delivering a package of Satisfaction. The New Emotion is studded with 21 jewels and is of the 42 hours of power caliber.

According to scientists, they have yielded discoveries that are widely acknowledged as important. The field has largely welcomed The New Emotion. The beta testers are unanimous: The New Emotion feature adding sound to the available set of expressions is the best thing that has happened in a long time. Purchase The New Emotion and Turn the tables on Satisfaction.

Pricing for The New Emotion will have the same recommended list / enduser price as the current innovative products that create powerful and effective branding programs for meeting the challenges and opportunities of The New Emotion based economy. Some multimodal presentation contents are produced in The New Version to show the effectiveness of The New Emotion function. The series will initially consist of three products: dynamic heart-shaped instruments of The New Emotion. The New Emotion represents the ideal package for Dependent Individual Clients (DICs). It offers full functionality at the high-end, including such advanced versions that show the effectiveness of The New Emotion expression function.

The New Emotion has something for every taste.

In case you do not like The New Emotion, with Toned arms and direct wired with the Smart Cable and Clever Clamp Combo, with a Clear Audio Aurora & Classic Variable Content, you can switch back which will clearly show you the effectiveness of The New Emotion Expression Function.

Featuring Varimotion technology, The New Emotion series, taken together with The New Emotion dynamics provides All the possibilities available. Once a Mood Algorithm is determined for The New Emotion two separate steps occur: firstly the Learning Process and the second consists of an Introduction to the Mood Algorithm Database.

This is the motto for The New Emotion: An interface is a necessary part of human-computer interaction, The New Version will show the effectiveness of The New Emotion function. Once a Mood Algorithm is determined for The New Emotion, two separate algorithms access the Database now updated to include support of The New Emotion.

Figure 1 shows the performance of musical individuals compared to the control groups of existing tests plus the results of The New Emotion test. If the customer becomes upset during the course of the call, his speech will change, and The New Pattern receives a different score for The New Emotion.

I do not expect it, The New Emotion, in spite of my training, I'll fail The New Emotion again, but I look for it now for a different reason.

The New I

In the St. Louis metropolitan area The New I will be introduced with new features and improved performance. The New I does not require… The New I. Features introduced in the design of The New I will be heavily influenced by the capabilities of a wide variety of systems. Resulting in The New Independence. The New Innovation. The New Incentive. The New Image. The New Icon. The New IQ. The New I.

The New I will provide a valuable Public service for the knowledge economy. Our first topic, is actually part of a larger set of changes going under the name of

The New I. This lesson will mostly talk about The New I package, detailing all the features of The New I currently in place. According to representatives from the Ocean, representatives from the Sun and representatives from the Channel, in their presentation entitled The New I Lives, The New I will lead development efforts with Questions, Exercises and Summaries.

Now that we've reviewed the classic approach, let's look at how The New I will work abstractly to solve the problems we've seen with the The New I. The editors of The New I have discussed the relaunch of The New I and its new format and focus, reducing objectionable content. What Should Parents Do About The New I? Watch Those Ads! and talk to their Kids about those Negative Ads. Perhaps the best indication of the sorry state of journalism these days is the acceptance of The New I.

There's a New (or Old?) I that looks to create an approach to the world of The New I niche which will feature connectivity, news and information. Work is The New I Solution of Choice. What does this mean? This year new systems are arriving with more information on The New I and the motivation behind it. Check this out: The New I is completely customisable by you!!! How do you do this? Just Click Replay. In the case of name changes, The New I must be made to reflect the name change and the The New I should inform the I-Center of the address to which The New I wishes to be addressed.

Central Highlights of The New I project include: the rebuilding and upgrading of all bridges, interchanges, and memory interfaces in St. Louis County. The blackout during the summer of 2003 proved that the critical infrastructure of The New I, eg, the power grid, is vulnerable. The New I will launch The New I Series with The New Series analysers, Name analysers, and The New Function analysers for use in the ambient world. Use of the The New I is the best present that can be offered, and the most advantages can be located in character-set support. The New I says, "Look at my record." The New I does not answer wild hypotheticals.

According to experts in the Department of The New I. You must first fill out a Request Form. Attach this form to the top of the documents required for issuance of The New I. It will take a minimum of five days after all, for the Future Hardware of The New I to arrive. Then, we'll put The New I shield in place. First we will

orient it as shown … Thus, The New I shield must be installed so that the two
big holes in the areas of buffer management and scalable network capabilities
correspond to The New I improvements made by the Missouri Department of
Transportation.

The New Love

According to Žižek, hate is The New Love; and Jesus said: "If anyone comes to me
and does not hate his father and his mother, his wife and children, his brothers, they
have not The New Love!" If you've ever read about The New Love, you've probably
encountered a well organized, good read, and The New Chapters on ethics and
jealousy are great. The New Love and Sex covers an enlarged view of The New
Works being accomplished by The New Love. The New Love holds the Secret to
Sustainable Intimate Relationships founded upon The New Love and Sex.

Introducing The New Love. Polyamory: The New Love Without Limits. The Sacred
Space Institute is a place for The New Love, with Tantra, Polyamory, The New Love
Without Limits, Viacreme, workshops, love, sexual healing, orgasms, sex and the
spirit. In The New Love study, researchers compared two sets of images, one taken
when the participants were looking at a photo of a friend, and the other when The
New Love was on a Boat with movie stars, TV personalities, Celebs, and more.
Introducing, The New Love: At some point it will become necessary to introduce
your man (forgive the gender). The New Love of my life. Isn't she glorious? She
arrived around noon today. I carefully disrobed her and then felt a bit guilty.

Hate Is The New Love, The New Love and Sex excerpted from The New Love and
Sex. The New Love Triangle—The Laptop Slides Into Bed, in Love… The New
Love and Sex. Lust Is The New Love when you're 29 years old, Female, living in
Long Island, New York, United States. Sticks & Stones May Break My Bones But
Whips & Chains Xite Me. The New Love Without Limits—Polyamory.

At some point it will become necessary to introduce your man (forgive the gender
bias, but hey! I'm a girl!). People who like The New Me also like The New Love
of my life. Say Hello to The New Love in My Life. Her name is Patina. I got one of
those dual core processors, so I'm curious how that'll work out. Also, I got a TV

tuner. Meet The New Year's Resolution on The New Love, we'll find The whole New Generation of songs about love. Each song, hand selected for its heartfelt expression. Hate Is the New Love. An ideologue is a person who believes very strongly in particular principles and tries to follow them carefully.

The New Media State

#2 Globally brand New Mexico as The New Media State. #3 Promote New Media business products and services to the local, regional, national, and international levels. #1 If an offer/answer/transaction succeeds, then The New Media State becomes active. I have never heard about a "proposed media state." If an offer/answer/transaction succeeds, The New Media State becomes active. I have never heard about a "proposed media state" . . . it isn't written anywhere.

All those people back East may one day get on the wagon train and become a citizen of The New Media State. And if they don't, many of their children will.

Despite the explosion of The New Media State, television, due to its monopoly and to the absence of an adequate system of press distribution is by far the media state. The New Media State is selected by incrementing the media state by 1 and the disk access parameters associated with The New Media State are set up. The New Media State, where now each media is hype-linked to sites related to the media context as well as to the user context. The user can now provide The New Media State of spelling as effectively as the opposite of the birth of printing—undoing the crystallisation of spelling, taking it back to The New Media State of fluid.

The New New Deal

The New New Deal reform pits reactionaries against progressives. The New New Deal also implies some major long-run spending. First, Social Security would pay all its accrued benefits all at once. To keep the United States solvent through the twenty-first century, we need to rethink Social Security, the tax structure, and health care.

Insurers have learned to pinpoint risks, and avoid them. With computer models that can test a quake's effects on your house there's no need for scientists. There is no sturdier liberal or Democratic slogan than "Jobs, jobs, jobs." But liberals have a problem: The old capitalist job-production machine is not just a well-planned reconstruction of The New Orleans. We need to set the stage for a comprehensive legislative initiative akin to The New Deal.

It's Time for The New New Deal.

…

Time for The New New Deal.

In three sections entitled "The Resilient," "Beyond Finance," and "The New New Deal," this speech draws heavily on a sense of history. The New New Deal is about Benefits alongside Bankruptcy. The New New Deal will create The New Republic of American Liberalism, the permanent majority party with The New Vision that goes by various names: the unowned society, The New Deal, and The New New Deal.

Following an incredible amount of volunteer labor hours and energy, this dream was realized when we at last saw the opening of The New New Deal Café where people drink coffee and tea they haven't payed for and are asked to simply stare into space all day. After three or four hours of this difficult, back-breaking labor, they're given another cup of coffee or tea in a to go cup—they are welcome to return after they've taken a good long nap.

The New New Deal is upon us. The president can either lead the charge or be run over by it. This upsurge will be called The New New Deal, and it presents a plan to deal with … The New New Deal! One of our greatest frustrations is when we collectively get wrapped up in theoretical discussions about The End of Reform and The New New Deal Liberalism in Recession and War. The New New Deal shows that President Bush's Social Security proposal is dead in the water—and that's a good thing, too. The plan was half-baked and fiscally speaking, without bankruptcy The New New Deal would just be The old New Deal in disguise. The New Republic of The New New Deal is original. It represents solid economic engineering and a straightforward Time of progress in The New Era of The New New Deal.

Where's The New New Deal? Where are the sweeping reforms that the Democrats
are all touting? They're nowhere. They can't even decide on a Presidential
candidate. Finally, The New New Deal will speculate on the degree to which The
re-crafted New Deal could serve as an organizing model for a liberal comeback of
The New New Deal. The New New Deal talks about The Rabbits Going Back in the
Hat, The Dance of the Crackpots, Welcoming the Enemy; and The Ride of the Wild
Rabbit—summarizing a wide variety of ambitious but viable projects to improve
all of our country by launching what's called The New New Deal—a multipronged
plan founded upon Bankruptcy—The New New Deal!

The New Republic of The New New Deal will be mindful of both the successes
and disappointments of The old New Deal of the 1930s. Conservatives and small-
government types are going to be run over by The New New Deal!

for Stan Apps

The New Night

Hello Everybody! I am happy to launch The New Night!

The New Night is a passage from one life to another.

To begin with, The New Night bears little relation to the television series I watched
with my grandmother. Father's mother and I saw The New Night full of other Skies
of other sizes: small, medium, large—completely original.

What The New Night does have, is the potential to be The New Night on the town.
The New Night rides like a movie in an egg, like a Fast Car. To take full advantage
of it, you should use nightclubs, food, drink, hotels and everything in between.
Take a Look at The New Night, the Sky! … The Night has been growing and
expanding.

Welcome to The New Night, the domain for the Passage of The Night.

The New Night is like a Leopard, a More compact, high quality night with
super fast, high resolution vision. The New Night has the Power of a Canon, the
equivalent of a Flash Shot into the Sky, fully original and it comes in all sizes: small,

medium, and large. The New Night will revolutionize bodybuilding by filling that crucial time Sweeping the Nation.

I think if the robbers are smart (and I hope they aren't) then they would be crazy enough to make the middle of the day The New Night. The all-nighter is The New Rite of Passage for young professionals. Who ever thought working so hard could be so much punch, so much life? In Manchester They don't live in the Sky, they live in The New Night.

The New Night is a time sequencing service. Herald Morning Sequencing, You are here: The New Night.

The New Night is Crib Swimming. At about 1 this morning, Zion started a full out crawl-stroke in its crib. My sister is in town for the weekend, and she offered to watch Adam if Beth and I wanted to go out for a while. In this respect, The New Night will bring legislation focusing on empowering women who are not interested in standard daytime jobs.

Ok cast/crew and viewers, hcrc is The New Night. Right off the bat, the filmmakers knew they wanted to cast Ben Stiller in the lead role of the hapless, yet ultimately heroic, Guard of The New Night. The New Night is not up to the standards of either series, but what show on television today is? If picked up, The New Night would be a part of the lineup and would be produced by Television. Alternatively, if performance is expected to improve with The New Night and The New Vision Capability, the comparison of night-versus-day from the previous stage must take place on a daily basis.

Network! Network! The New Night has gone from TV to comics and back again.

Are weekends becoming too expensive? How to make your date without breaking the bank. The New Night is a program at the Museum of New York's American Museum of Natural History which has been so popular that all available dates have sold out. Attila the Hun and his pals exhibit creatures up top, like the 20th Century Fox, and make things a bit tense for The New Night. I don't think the show was all that bad, but I really wish it had been given more time to find The New Night.

The New Night follows a circular path that goes toward the Sacramento River on West Sacramento Avenue, down Nord Avenue and then The New Night goes downtown. The New Night is the official time of Rembrandt—Rembrandt Harmenszoon Van Rijn is generally accepted as the most important Dutch to Watch The New Night from Year to year, focusing on the release of light walking through The New Night.

The New Pantoum

Jolly Teabags! The New Pantoum doesn't need it's oil changed! Imagine that! The New Pantoum is an Amazing lubricant.

The New Pantoum is The topical New Challenge, the Previous Topic was La Pixie Strangiato. The Challenge challenged Duration. The New Topic will be Alone.

I copied The New Pantoum and placed it in The New Pantoum. I've just created this—Enjoyed it.

And The New Pantoum doesn't need its oil changed! Imagine that!

The New Pattern Poem

There is a brief summary for production and rhythm of The New Pattern Poem, and a statement that The New Pattern Ci and Qu are among the metrical verse.

The New Quatrain

This is also the ihh sound which occurs in each line of The New Quatrain and gives it a lighter, singing tone lending a continuity to the preceding quatrains. The New Quatrain illustrates the poet's neutrality vis-a-vis the subject. Those who keep their reason but lie to the clouds by denying them—Stanza fifteen is also revised—pave the way for The New Quatrain. The poet sought the ear of Christ on these mad things. And then in the white pavilion when the poet, with the old remark about gleaning abandoned, put The New Quatrain about the greedy master in place—What had happened in the meantime? It was The New Quatrain consisting of four phrases in a column shape. The New Quatrain and logo have been used this year in The New Inauguration. And now, take the Now out of line 17, starting The New Quatrain with 'The day.' Other than those two minor things, it was a very well written poem. Some of The New Quatrain pieces are opulent and highly detailed. The New Company, which specializes in accurate reproductions of grand antiques has brought The New Quatrain. Usagi spoke as she was thinking about The New Quatrain of the prophecy. "I don't know Usagi-san." Hotaru spoke, "indeed they would like to remove The New Quatrain. Ours, as well as The New Quatrain just given, also deals with the Pope changing countries (and possibly the Church), Roman guards in torment/panic, clouds nuclear.

The New Rejection Letter

Regarding the appended "observations," which are called "the principal reasons" for the rejection, are e-mails The New Rejection Letter or should these also be regarded as a sign that these folks actually have me in the "watch for the future" pile? You got The New Rejection Letter, which translated means: Your domain sucks, why did you submit it to GreatDomains? Please do not do it again. It also said something about "so what does everyone think about The New Rejection Letter?" I remember getting "excited" at first because I thought… Now I'm not saying this right, but with this being the email age, not responding to your email is The New Rejection Letter. I have responded to many ads from the Appeals committee, but their concerns about the wording in The New Rejection Letter were out of hand—their Discussion focused only on the second paragraph. In The New Rejection Letter one finds a similar statement.

The New Sapphic

The New Sapphic: Some Like It Hot.

Among The New Sapphic fragments of special interest are the beautiful "ostrakon ode," a simple poem on feminine attire.

The Independent Cinema has brought The New Ethnicities into the Hall of Critical Dialogues. The world of Independent Film and Video has made The New Sapphic into a series! Some Like It Hot: The Cinema of The New Sapphic.

Click here to get a Full Version of The New Sapphic. Download The New Sapphic. In addition also get the latest Applications, Tv Shows, Movies, and Games.

So the days multiply, caught here in the devil's windpipe, where winds hoot. (See The New Sapphic, unwrapt out of mummy's rags.) I have information on The New Sapphic sex, The New Sapphic sex is best! I have seen all the Internet… Anything.

The New Sprung Rhythm

Consonant with the solemnity of the theme and capable also of modulation without abruptness into a different measure, that is The New Sprung Rhythm.

The New Subjectivity

Craft has traditionally been interpreted as a combination of individual creativity and closeness to materials or making. The New Craft or My World of The New Subjectivity turns to craft as a way of seeing beyond the global product framework that valorized The New Subjectivity of the warrior [which served to recast women as being of the home-front]. The emergence of The New Subjectivity in contemporary design, as designers use sophisticated new technologies to do their work, is strongly informed by their distinct but complementary backgrounds. The New Subjectivity senses that private feelings are always related to collective feelings.

The term 'Rosie the Rivetor' changed in social and literary sensibilities in the mid-seventies as manifested in the Greens, The New Subjectivity, and reactions to consumer society. The New Subjectivity briefly recalls the "nine-year process from the beginning" that resulted in The Love Tapes and Films which were only precursors for The New Subjectivity on display in documentary film and video of the 1980s and 1990s. In literature, the nimbus surrounding these decades was termed The New Subjectivity. Historically, the familiar evaluations haven't included The New Subjectivity and the same fate has befallen them as befell the Soviet regime in the 1980's which failed to respond to The New Subjectivity.

English industrial Structuralism and The New Subjectivity, today create a space where it is common to be told that whatever is said is no more than The New Subjectivity. The failure of The New Subjectivity lies not merely in its vehicle. Certainly, lyrics like "Once I cave in, what can I fight? I can never win My World" show The New Subjectivity in its Design phase. In addition to being quite mystical, The New Subjectivity becomes a God-like presence that creates The New World. The logic here can be quite contradictory, particularly around debates on the emergence of The New Subjectivity.

The New Subjectivity created through ascetical practice may come about, but The New Subjectivity will more likely result from The New Social Relations and The New Symbolic artistic direction in the Contemporary Arts. Society must be capable of forming collective agencies of enunciation that match The New Subjectivity, in such a way that it desires its own mutation. This will give us a glimpse into The New Subjectivity of humanity, which replaces the liberal humanist subjectivity of Enlightenment-based modernity.

The technology of the self, proposed as The New Subjectivity, is not a marginal phenomenon one finds only in evidence among members of the art world. Functioning as a linguistic marker coined originally by journalists, The New Subjectivity wasn't simply more rewarding than earlier forms of subjectivity, what was important was the moral prism. The New Subjectivity looks not only at negative performances (rejecting wealth or sexuality), but primarily toward the positive articulation of The New Subjectivity that would be refracted accordingly. The New Subjectivity doesn't want to be aimed at the "lucky minority of the well-informed."

Among the many formulations used to Assume a subject, The New Subjectivity is the entrance and the awareness that makes The New Subjectivity that which we are trying to describe and invent at the same time. Attention thus becomes a fluctuating, floating dimension attached to The New Subjectivity that it also helps define.

Here's something New: you're reading an essay on The New Subjectivity.

The New Subjectivity, I conclude, is characterized by hybridity, delirium, automatism, and a troubling ambiguity between the self and its technological process. I also have a new house in Connecticut, and I'm going to buy a car and be multiple, and finally be replaced by The New Subjectivity of postmodernism spawned on the Internet, the main representative of cyberspace.

The New Unrequited Love

I think for me The New Unrequited Love represents a man who I feel I can be me with, and who wants me for who I am, not 'what I can do.' The New Unrequited Love! Maniacs in Manhattan! More Than Usual, I Mean! For those of you in NYC, the much-anticipated, the long-awaited… The New Unrequited Love.

The New Villanelle

(Not that some of them aren't still bad, The New Villanelle in particular, but that's life.) And to top the news off, until I find out about my IP, I'm just gonna have to talk about me. For a while I knew someone / Who made me feel complete / Smiling now though she is gone / For a while she was the one / Who simply swept me off my feet.

The New War

This week marks the anniversaries of three landmark events that paved the way for Recent Developments. With all the fuss about Barack Obama and Hillary Clinton, John Edwards's presidential campaign might look like a long shot. So, at this time there is a little relief and we have a pleasant topic instead of The New War.

The National Press Club in Washington, D.C. presented a discussion Forum on Religion and Public Life delivering nonpartisan, timely information on issues and debates related to religion, news, politics, and The New War. Justin Akers is active in antiwar and cross-border solidarity work. He is the author of "A Draft in the Air? The Just War Tradition, Terrorism and The New War." He said The New War is actually against three enemies: the religious rulers of Iran, the "fascists" of Iraq and Syria, and Islamic extremists like al Qaeda.

Being Right is The New War… on Freedom.

The New War is The Web of Crime That Threatens America's news, analysis, commentary, interactives, photos, video, audio and web resources. If you're the editor of a [dot]org and a columnist for FoxNews[dot]com, there is only one scenario for American success in Iraq—and it won't be easy. The World is a free, open, video streaming web site that provides on-demand video of The New War as well as live feeds of Social Drinking—Balko, Balko, Cato, Radley… Boo.

The New War… on Freedom.

Moved into the Sidebar now, Reflections on the American Occupation—It's time for the Navigation Home, time to pack it in, draw up a Synopsis, thank the Cast & Crew, kick back and write a Novel about the whole thing, maybe do a couple Radio Broadcasts. Security will come in the form of Books about John Kerry by John Kerry. Unfortunately, the world keeps coming up with things for The New War, like Terror, Technology and Culture, for, um… example.

The New War… on immigrants.

Preventing The New War and Social Drinking, part of Our Special Coverage will be taken in moderation, including an hourlong documentary examining the Home Market for Wargames, Predictions, Military Discussions, Military Jokes and The New War. Special Report: The New War in the Middle East is The New War in the Middle East is The New War, a powerful warning that global crime is robbing us not only of our Most important goals in The New War, but also of keeping our sights set on the globe.

The New War… on Poverty.

The Back Door to international Terrorism is ineffective and counterproductive when implemented incrementally—one, two, three, four, five, six, seven… ah, ha, ha… eight, nine, ten years after the Sept. 11 terror attacks. With the steady erosion of our basic rights, we're in danger of becoming driven by people's interests and their seedy well-being and by putting an end to poverty "as we know it."

The New War… on poverty. The New War… on The Poor.

Covering the New War in the weeks since the death of America, a haunting rumor Running totally amok about how much money has been spent in the current year arose out of a deluge of Revisionist materials from the Institute for Historical Revision.

Read first-hand accounts by journalists covering the war in Afghanistan, A Tragedy of Pearls. On April 25, 1898 the United States declared war on Spain following the sinking of the Battleship Maine in Havana harbor on February 15, 1898.

from Tanka

Kaethe Schwehn

Tanka to Me

Draw my breath,
you're bending

flexy. In this mishap
are my shelves, rain

buckled trunk. Home
has no grassy arms

only cracks worn into
quail bowls.

Rhyme shoal with everything.

Tanka to Me

Try gentle.

Remember how tasty a
sandwich can be?

Sandblast your poems.
Start over.
The world's not any better
for Dover Beach.

There's a bitch trying
to write you a parking ticket.

Right where you thought
you'd be safe.

Think of the turtle
that appeared on your sun deck.

How the dog went mad
inside the house.

How she scratched her claws
against the windows.

How the turtle
didn't care. Ahh… wet
wood said the turtle inside
her head.

When Tanka Is Happy

When Tanka is happy the chariot
begins to roll. The twin beasts
bow their heads and puke.
The puke smokes
when Tanka is happy.

When Tanka is happy, God
cups her chin in her hands.
God puts her elbows on the
railing and sighs.

Then cardinals sprout pins.
Tanka drills her fist
through glass shepherds

and the confirmands gather
her up in their arms.
When Tanka is happy

her eyes are wicks.
Winter mews. Books say
she was found in a vein,
trancing with cavespeak, rioting

against convex circumstance.
When Tanka is happy she sprouts
yam bands at her pinnacle.
Look at her.
Look at you when Tanka is happy

frilled radii bronzing at your core.

No Tanka and Briar Report Today

I can say nothing of Tanka and Briar today
except they are possessed.

There is nothing you can do for the two of them today.
You must go away with your microphones,
with your camera vans and jogging strollers.

It is coming into them, this sky:
spring Dakota storm, sore green blossoming.
It is coming in right here.

Tanka as Sixteen Angels Bestowing Attributes

Angel one grafts snow below the baby's
face and the baby's face glistens.

Tires hiss and angel two grafts mandrake
roots into the baby Savior's arms.
The Savior screams.

Angel three grafts the slip of bowling lanes into the Savior's smile.
Angel four anchors Dallas cow haze in the armpits, moisture
mucked between reddening hairs. The Savior won't smell
himself like this until he gets lost inside the temple.
Then the scent will come, rising up, familiar
as the sacrificial belle's beating heart brought before
her dying eyes. What eyes our Savior had that looked

and looked, past his mother's face into the opening doors into
the gale and the pedometers, the ax's thrust, the pedant's cowl
stained with pizza sauce. The Savior saw his own hand on a woman's cheek, cupping
at her breast, his own hand pulling a dead man up by the scruff of his neck, the dead man's
screams molded tart in the dark hall, how afterward the Savior
touched his body as though it had been scalded everywhere.

Me to Tanka

Tanka, it is
me walking the beach
among the dead bodies
of squid, their half-lemon
eyes inked black, getting in no sun.

The serpents twinning below the sand
dune their bodies up. I climb one and sit beside
a patch of grass. Tanka, it occurs to me that this
is a heaven beach. The sheet of silver sky
and the sheet of silver water compliment
each other.
                "Nice ribs," says the sky.
                "Cute hairpins," says the sea.

The hairpins are thin white
bombs and the belly of the sea
explodes. Sand prickles the face of the sky.

The sea was being facetious, which I didn't think
was allowed in heaven.
Tanka, it is.

Tanka as Ark

Tongue lolling,
the llama lounges in her thigh.
She repeats words the llama likes:
rickshaw, Sudan, task, muskwort, llama.

Where her wrist veins cross
a dove's eye opens.

A sherry-dipped slug at every joint, hawk
feathers in her blisters, snake spine chinned, kiss
of rooster in her cough, rodent body
rippling through jaw.

Seahorses curl at her temples.

Squinting through a seaweed ruckus, the otters
in her calves, sleek in motion, quicken toward
the bullfrogs in her thighs,
hiccupped throats turned inward.

> Sometimes she breaks leaves in the gutter
> until the menagerie is quiet.
> Until the distance thickens.

The Mourning Cloak is a butterfly
inside her heart and it is dead.
    Its scales shine.
     One antennae doubled over by the wind.
    White sunk along the lower wing.
The other animals do not bother it.
To have a dead thing in the heart is sacred.
    Come, let's have the tongs and bones.

The sun is the mouth of a jar
and inside the jar is a lion.

from **Sin is to Celebration**

Amanda Ackerman / Harold Abramowitz

Love Song from a Slightly Sour Lyre

[
        (pouring tea)
"For I have always loved
"Poetry, and found in poets
"Some finer grain
"Lacking in the Common Herd,
"As you will agree."
        Whereupon
Picking up the lemon
Cream, and sugar,
And with a trill of fluttering laughter
        (like water over a dike)
The young one turned to me
        Saying:

                ]

[

                ]

[   ]

[

                ]

[   ]

Love Song from a Slightly Sour Lyre

And said the one
        (pouring)
"For I have always loved
finer grain, you
picking lemon, sugar,
And a trill of (water
over a dike)

The young one turned to me
        Saying:
"I? Why I should like nothing more
Fair, than to be
Shock And reproach.
Some swan
And rapidly more meadows"

But I, with precision
of quiet thought
splashing feet first
Into the lake,
        Frightened.

Lake?
Which?

Why this lake;
The lake of absolute
        Indicate

Love Song from a Slightly Sour Lyre

And said
(pouring)
"have always loved
"and found
"Some finer
"Lacking
"As you will
Whereupon
Picking up
and
and with a trill of laughter
(like water)
The one turned to
Saying:
"And you, my
"What would you like?

"nothing
"Fair
"in the forest
"of your

Shock

And
Some
Confronted with

me?

And
Of, more meadows
But
Went through meadows

of more quiet
And
the lake
Frightened

Lake?

lake?

lake;
The lake

Indelicate!

Poem

[

                ]

[

                ]

The core goes in the garbage can
            I went down to tinsel town
The core goes in the garbage can
            Someone was shoving nickels
The core goes in the garbage can
            into a juke box.
Awaiting the collector.

Poem

down
went down
A broken jug
Someone was shoving
Too long
Into a box
In its own fire.

Sometimes there are
The faces
Bobbling bumbling
painted color
On a string
for a dime.
on a string
my doll my
Step right
Doll, the night
Twists
All
gives full
If your arm
Money's worth
off and shatter
Come look
Grinding
The seedless
wax shine in
of red
of honey;
and even broken
Forcing a moment's
over
into

out
of
on the line.

The core goes in
went down
The core goes in
Someone was
The core goes in
into a box
awaiting.

Poem

The sun fell
       I down to tinsel
A half broken enamel jug
       Someone was
Too long
       in a
juke In its own fire.

Sometimes there are
       Bobbling On a string
Three for a dime
       Night on a string
       my my doll

right folks

The night squirms, twists
       All round a song
She gives her full
       your plaster arm
Money
Doesn't
       fall off and shatter

Come look
       the apple
Ten million wire
       sculptures look the
apple Grinding the seedless apple

       The was shine in
Of brightest red
       of perpetual broken mirror

forcing a moment's pleasure
              a microsecond hazed out
For ten on the line

The core goes in the
              I went down to tinsel
The core goes in the
              Someone was shoving the core
In a juke
              awaiting

Orpheus in Transit

[ ]

For as the camel later said:
"That desert was absurd.
"It had far too many of *raisons*
"Not enough ice cream,
"And only one song bird

]

[ ]

[

]

Transit

the camel later said:
"That desert was absurd
it had far too many *raisons* ice cream,
and only one song bird.
I unpacked my hump
and left behind a trinket
Which you grieve into a
genuine $3.98 Basement

The lion sat in its fire
And its eyes And fangs And claws
Were Red when it spoke
its voice monogrammed
like a Ronson lighter.
And said:
          "rebellion!
                    anarchy
burn the flame

Two children sat in a tree With books
the wind Reading between
the comments
One liked the face
one liked the page
But both shook
hearts That picnics in season
Would prove rage

Orpheus in Transit

1.

for
that desert
it had
not enough
and only one
to square
therefore:
and left, behind that is
magic silver
which
will grow into
imported oasis ($3.98
at the basement)

2.

the lion sat in its circle
and its eyes
and its fangs
and its claws
red in a circle
    it spoke
was the tongue
and angels, and voice
lighter
and said:
    "it must be"
like that
and laughed

3.

a tree
the wind
reading the lines
and making comments
eyes
face
one liked the page
but both agreed
(and)
that
and that
    like despair
would prove only rage

The Kites of Fall

The kites of fall
bob & weave
dancing through leave flights
and the V of birds

]

The Kites of Fall

kites of fall
    & weave
dancing through
and the V of birds
headed south for winter
In the streets
washed by rain
run,
following with silver strings
the sharp clear
of the kite

The Kites of Fall

        fall & weave
through leave flights
and the birds
        south
the winter in the streets
        rain following with strings
clear of the kite

from **Sketches**

Jaye Bartell

Sketch: Sharon Massachusetts

blear window's other-side
       pace of train
allows tree line pave streets
fence links and cloud swarm
to form
 place singular
       tinged
with drab
   and easiest
temperament.

To plainly look
       the unspooling scape
       late May green
froth top (sky) with drear

feel as a marsh
soggy posts throughout
with bird huts atop
raised and hospitable for

      song
      birds
     a singer
     who then
      sings.

Sketch: Quincy

shingle and

shingle and

bricks
and

windows

these seen
make place

detail amassed
woven so one
could live inside

The mean is not other
than the composition

Sketch: MBTA Holbrook

hill of tassel reeds
        will block
        will block
passed then   slat fence
        seen through to
    brick places
        trees afield
streams.

Disobey your structure
        fall into the water
way, made of topples and
    lost.

Sketch: South Station

Lamppost. Lamp.
Inveterate, there.
Like a bridge.
To use.
Or not use.

Sketch: T Tunnel

flick, view
            procedure
flick, view
            procedure

flicks, viewed, proceed
speed
                increase
voluble
            several aspects
show a faster
                quickening

steady   metric
        shrill

steadily metrically
appropriately matched

Sketch: Tennessee Dawn

hanging
       over
 the Holston
       the moon
still there
       at dawn
after
       evening
  dawn

tucked in
       mountains
the moon
       hanging
       over
over the
  Holston
after evening
hanging
       over
over
the Holston

  the moon
hanging over

Sketch: Fullerton, CA

Slumber,
       fog beset beasts,
sleep—
       chance the sky,
changed, will not restore
tones before known
hills of Fullerton, California   didn't wake up
Let the pines   *quill*   go dull

Madrone's fleshed peelings
       run the ridge with
   palms
dirt mounds
several varieties of
     bizarre weeds

A haze, grime city sent   or sea fog?
California ground,
steaming,   sleeps

Sketch: Montana

Beige reeds remain leaned
from press of snow
receded, changed now to
rain. The season shifts,
comes to fade the white
cold until bare land again
shows, it is mud and stones,
red and variously jagged.

There spreads vastly such
terrain unattended, to see down
from a bridge, a river of green
continuity, a wire fence
along a hill, plane of hummocks
that roil into view as waves
of unmoving land, however
tender in the thaw.

Out of the mountain's severity
into the prairies, a town
across a field, trailers, piles of
tires, pyres, overturned bags
of garbage, fence posts, reeds,
unify amid increased wind,
stimulus of being again among heaps
of rusted metal, of our world.

Move of wind brushes grass
to gain shape and beige.
Terms of color betray gradation
furrowed tones risen and sunken.

. . .

The Pines
>for Brandon Shimoda

If the river ceased moving
it would freeze, or would have
in winter, if winter. It's March,
a day from equinox, and though
snow remains in the valley, it's
residual. A sudden red pine
flashes into view—dried to that
color, dead, but yet to fall. What
other pines there are,
and there are many,
remain upright, staunch
in the cloudy morn.

Montana Morning

Smoke or
mist arising from
within the pines
hovering, a cloud—
or from a fire,
someone waking,
wakening, down
from rounded balds,
making place to
take place.

Once a substance
permutable a vapor
could drift in air

happens sometimes
forms to solidity like
glass *can* break

and rising too swiftly
does break.

Rightly Moving

Rightly moving
with the river
it's bank a
gulch of rough
rough redstone,
gradations of brown
of mountains of land
the valleys fitting the
river-shaped rivers.

Rain on the Grasses

Rain on the grasses
matted and down
leaning at the close
of the season of snow.

Sketch: Western Massachusetts Building / Rail Area

might be that time (generality)
        is saturation
of the Heywood Shoe building
or a steeple higher than factories
        and a pigeon
            goes through
whence the same sky
        remaining there.

Distant stacks
        and made
            a haze
by distance
        stacks!

Old fences
        elder brick shacks, smoke stacks
pigeons and slab windows it's
not always ending or
        yet over
horizon's obscurations.

Sketch: National Ethos

"Country" is terminology
            whereas fence's
posts   wires taut
            are material specifically
vagrant shrubs   streams of water

as additional examples—

Abolish that term
            our families,
(even us, alone)
            go home
slumber, un-encompassed
            no matter.

Fields of rows of plants
in May, yet manifest
partial and glaringly striving,
or those roadways
            tracks of dirt
for access
            a single (humanly)
inedible berry—

            lose these, a view-
            ethic, and give
            allegiance
            to hard colors
            not present
            in a typical swath
            of mid-continent.

Sketch: Hudson Marsh

Marsh
I fall
in mind
all the
time

a pole
in mud
holds the line
from somewhere to
somewhere else.

Sketch: Down the Mtn.

Brindled hills
          maroon rises
of maroon
          rising
November and
  it's jackets!
          wrap us
in your hills
like your hills
of maroon.

Sketch: Dean

of the
    taste
how to
    taste
obdurate
 tremors

Crumble of
    plaster
crumbling in
   a closing
  hand

heavy the lids
heavy them
eyes lower
the shading
over eyes
see
   churn
forgive
   languor

And as a paper
     torn
the whole
rips
   stops
     quiet

Cortland

Jessica Smith

a conversation
intense as the sun

                    look away
                    into red
                       fields

                    cortland

                    barns and sunset converge

                    look over you

read   red-faced
   is   seat

            driver
twi   passenger   ed

       I cannot see your eyes

everything
in sight

green and red green or red
the car the grass
the apples your eyes

we are not
crying

a pound of red globes
bumped and bruised and
cut   while

story-telling

next and next and next

                              annexed:

the next day i bought a new red coat
and walked to the coop
filled my pockets with pink ladies
and did not walk home

from **Boxelder**

David Pavelich

Consumed, the fence

of strings address

of crickets *admit*

accomplishment, I

and gradual

hail of dogwood keys

Neighbor, the fit interference

figure between them

and one source

on two paths cast

the interference fit

a pattern, *a dish*

of blue glass, fit

their reflections

in reluctance to go there

The proper rain

with folded hands

a map of strings

or memory of orange

scent in the skin

of strings, of digits, one

and watching seen none

this problem of leaves

both of them transparent

ready for an extract, crawled

the chrysanthemum, the aster

by a firefly

but anticipate the ending

I would if strength

was a relationship

colors, and tolerance

not a present rain but rain

from an earlier storm

together when you find

there as in turn is like

the whole thing was a kind

of conversation

Despite the day it loses

the clover's line

or louder and softer sounds

confused by

touching, lowering

a cloud of houseflies

the effect of new

leaning, contained in

everyday the unwrapping

of another seed

a crib, a suspended basket

are unknown to me

for a crowd of fuchsia blooms

dropping, and be able that sometimes

grateful, but, the blue

who lives here now, behind

This is someone's

backyard

All of this belongs

to someone,

followed,

each seed

a combination

But we have nine

tonight, three

red, one

the color

of my hands, five

a string-of-pearls

in the picture

window

but hopes all ten

grow in the casement

the lights

by curtains

the air

by screens

cannot open

my hands

of dry paper

because was anyone

the wall's

embroidery

the shadow

of begonia, twisted

unstitched

the picture

For what we know

is the last time

this has been

and attempts before

arriving,

in full evidence

a stack of yellow-

green color

to get the wind

came alive, was calm

it does in,

refused but won't end—

and the avenue is green

into light,

is black into clouds

or blue swims the dark

is purpose a life—

for March

of, for,

people who stand

in the street of our warming

Ours is forgotten

family

posts, wire

in the clay

like the smell

of tea

of the afternoon

is still asleep

the spider

comes in, the housefly

that stress

against screens,

fence and trees

into leaning

gift, fair, right,

or close an opening

that opens out

on the treble of means——

a set that contains

the diamond mesh

of a neighborhood

of the afternoon

[Bestiary With A Broken Window &
A Thin Though Not Unkind Smattering Of Light]

Erin M. Bertram

I. Leaning On The Limits Of Myself

Dear—,
        I understand this body only as much
As I understand the vined brick exterior of certain
Abandoned buildings.
                A doe, one flank littered
With buckshot, starts, stumbles, shifts her weight
Ridiculously in a wildly labored plea.
                        What else to reach for
When the reaching, the very act of it,
Itself comprises the knowing?
                  Time turns over & over
On itself, dives to the bottom, comes up
For air, paces the living room, culling creaks
From otherwise subtle floorboards.
                    One relentless ocean,
Deep & always breaking. The gulls in their frenzy.
A single boat nodding on the shore.
                  Today I am writing
& writing letters, & the grey hint on the wall
Where once in a panic I killed a gypsy moth, its form
Held there, suspended in silhouette.
Take this as a sign.
           Today I am writing
& writing letters. One for weight,
What it means to catch & hold a thing,
& mean it. One for the delicate assemblage of birds.
And one for you:
           Dear—,
When the tulip trees drop their blossoms,
The thump is unmistakable. For the last three days,
I've woken to rain
              Slapping the window by my head.
There is more than one way to find sanctuary.
Would that my shadow were at least as big
As my body.

II. Magpie Eager, Magpie Still

Steel wool & stain, the body prefers
            benediction. Where span of wing without fledge?
      Without cowardice, where fluster & eventual (brief) flight?

As when the magpie splays its throat
            to the world. As what is broken goes fixed
      only in the sewn & sewn field of memory. A woman pulls a sweater——

                  fraying, frayed——over her neck & shoulders,
      mutters *anathema, amphora* hushed & on end.
The way the mahogany chair just sits there. On the cutting board

      a knife serrated, left unengraved without intent.
      The tang, sheathed, how long has it been
                        since the walls began to hum?

      Cardiac infrastructure a bellows early evening.
            Nearly misgiving, *nearly* meander
                  blindfolded in an open field of wolvery,

cursory gone the way of instinct, instinctual as an excuse,
                  though less than forgivable. The way the eyes stare blind
      as what is meant, ultimately, to divide, does.

III. Hoop Snake Reverie

A broken window. Digitalis. Rooks descending
on the lawn.

What you cannot see won't hurt you.

The way it moves,
                  all those tiny muscles arching in unison, nearly sickens me,
turning the soil with each sudden wheel
                        of its slick & agile body.

Colts in a field burgeoning, feeble & full of light.

Constellations, mid-afternoon, equally crouched & on fire.

That day pigeons flapped wildly, the bedroom window
rubbed too clean to see—
                    an unmistakable sound.

When the sun goes down, all I can do is work it back up.

The wicked collapse in the corn,
                    all others line up against the brickest of walls.

This, knee deep in turgid water, is also called consolation.
Current around our ankles.

We will never sleep
                    so long as wolves roam the yard at night.

A pumpkin in the bassinet.

Bike stolen fifty feet from your bed. And back behind
the garage, honeysuckle, sunflower,
                    vertebrae bleached clean through.

There is a gentle hum in the floor.

Some tired inaudible expression.
Something senseless making love to itself on end.

   IV. My Tattoo

Something worth naming as yet without a name.
What's to be said for a bird paused in eternal alight
on forearm, wings spread both away & in embrace?

My paramour. Event horizon. The flesh the first
& quietest defense. Which is not to say insignificant
or any less than other, more hardy variants of armor,

whose weight is implied or otherwise & otherly
borne. Lines sketched, drawn, traced, then memorized,
fingered nights, mornings wildly admired. Once

embossed, the flesh rises in either protest or accord;
what else is to be expected, what response better suited
to dignify such intrusion. Forearm gone all Byzantine

relief, firebird affixed, you rise, a tiny Christ, held
there by layers thin as paper sheaves. Creature born,
creature risen, creature risen again. That Sunday,

under the whirring buzz of mechanized & flourishing
ink, my body held there, willingly, for minutes
at a time. Bird of pyre, bird of soot, bird of cigarette

gone rococo, gone smolder, fixed intaglio, most intimate
intarsia. Wingspan flared feral, silent suspension
between alight & arrival, always impending, always

already there. And its plumage, tenacious, tender
feathers of the neck exposed, and exposé on what it is
to be humble & brazen, &, yes, deservedly holy. Forever

turning in on itself, turning over & over, a face turned
away & quickly back again. As when thick stone wears
the abrasions given it by wind or the beloved palm,

a vestigial translation of its former self. That requisite
turning, effectual in its want, until final swift—
inevitable?—release, sole blue beacon of an eye

amid a whirl of otherwise dynamic, unchanging heat.

V. Tremolo

The year you wrapped a beehive in string, it resembled a single
Head, bandaged, bodiless, hung from a branch reached

Only with sure-footing & the ladder behind the collapsing shed.

On the porch, I waited slack-jawed & charmed, as you drew the string taut,
Then cinched it quick with a bowline we'd both learned

From your hand-me-down Boy Scout handbook. The hive shook its head,

A tantrum of bees plotting their escape, hunger in terrible frenzy.
It swayed from its branch—peeling birch, as if a wallet

Stuffed with receipts had had enough, each white sheaf turning slowly

Away from the weather-beaten trunk—until finally it gave, with a sudden,
Though not unforeseen, snap. For an instant, it was a confused

Balloon of papier maché. On impact, the hive cracked, egg-like, calving

Hundreds of buzzing bodies scatter-shot in as many directions. I ran.
Any other day, they'd dive, unabashed, into the gilt throat of tiger lilies,

Hum deep into swollen bleeding hearts, thrum the insides of even the shiest

Violet. The stir would be nearly erotic & just as irredeemable.
Instead, I could make out a swarm of red flashing lights, the white sheet,

You, limp-eyed, roaming the driveway, barking at the air.

. . .

Ecstatic immolation. The delicacies of fireside contraband.

This is what was meant when God made the 4th of July,
Or so kids say, reassuring one another that the tinder boxes

In their fists are ready to open in grace. The box elder boasts a piñata.

Iced tea soaks in the sun. The whistle of bratwurst & steak searing
On the grill. Toss gristle to the dogs, get right down to the bone,

Quick. Bottle rockets an abbreviated form of arson—

The way it would hiss at her, the way her face would bloat,
Eventually calm itself in time to watch the irises slump, then wither.

Each petal a withered scrotum—lavender, wrinkled, thinning—

Shed without mercy. She would discover eye shadow. Blush.
A sparrow skein raucous overhead. Each season, the scars would

Recede, specters of their former selves. This, the recovery room.

VII. You Said To Be Ruined

By desire, & I said wouldn't that be nice. I said the air in this room is like a
thousand tiny tongues, then tapped out the only song I knew on the upright
piano fiercely out of tune. You watched as the streetlight cut you in two.

I think someone died here, you said, & I felt the weight suspended on a
rusted chain sway behind my sternum & drop to my belly fast & without
warning.

Body as a machine, body as a plan, body scrolled & unscrolled. Body left out
in the rain.

To stand with you in a darkened room & count the ghosts swimming
beneath us. Between us. To lift my head to the dirty ceiling &
my other hand on your collarbone,
the one you broke when you were three days old.

In the drawer of a secretary, spoons taken by verdigris, postcards stamped but
never written, a crucifix on the belly rubbed to sheen. Misericorde.
Misericorde.

Murder Poems

Laura Sims

See the Pines

That are

"Such as they are"

And the ones that escaped

There were horrors

Then horrors

Were stacked onto those

What have *you* done?

Nothing——

Grafted, shaved

This one was brand new

(For a minute)

What made me

Do

Everything

Down

And

Red.

I'm controlled, I am not doing

Interviews. Still

In the marble halls

I forgot

*

My sweatshirt stained with blood

It's winter

I fear

I've committed a crime

I woke up and asked, *Where's*

my mother?

*

I first hold snow

Its molecular structure—

Time

For my personal
History?

I remember the hammer, but not the bottle
of wine

They kept getting up

Then the man lay down, I believe

What

Lighted the wine

Frail, the man
Standing
After the mishap in the hut

He goes into a *shaking fit* or *magazine store* to calm his nerves.

She flushes him out
Bellied up to the ruins
He crafted

What's mine is mine, "what's mine is mine," *what's mine is mine.*

Clumps
Form over the twin rust birds—
We can't say
Whether it's *clouds* or *smoke*
Or *snow* (Without which things would be: glossy, immaculate, only his life)

And her sandals are left.

The Shape lifts & devours it whole: her hair, bones and robe

Even the necklace they told her would last and last and last

*

A woman is crouched by the meat

She takes her face from her long blue sleeve

"which therewith became like unto an egg"

*

And the yam-seller, too:

Looks up with

"Fouled with blood and foam and clay"

*

It is no accident

No, rather, I am still here

Because she was in my life, we

*

Under debris	On Mt. Solo	Snagged on the banks of a creek
Off a logging road	Down a ravine	Lomas de Poleo
The Dumpster next door	Otter Lake	Or The sea floor
The plains of	The desert	Or out in In any case

There

*

When we woke   A whole planet of waste

I left the planet

To itself

And found instead

Her living room

I hit the street with nothing

Yet "ferociously"

Her head

Assailed

The planet

Kept us safe from one another and

It stung

It spun me off——

I fed the good boy peanuts and threw peanuts at the bad

What matters is where that part of her goes

What matters is where that part of her goes (her empty

cavities glistened). A beautiful girl is a beautiful girl is a

beautiful greenish in color. I did sprinkle salt on the parts

thereof, 'til the rings did glisten'; her heels revealed she'd

been hoisted. Her hair was long, and: the longer the hair.

Cared for and spoon-fed her just deserts, she wore a good

shape, 'she was good in all ways'; there will be more dirt,

more money, no dirty talk, no more nutrition.

My god is this a man

I rode around and rode around
The middle of the world

I cleaned myself
A bottle and inside

She fell on top of me
Shocked, the human beings

I lied her on the floor
I said, "I lied her on the floor"

I don't
I don't deny (I wasn't there) but

I'd had the dearest little dream

I was good
Or good enough
And careful

It was
Both
Fell backward on the bed
And she became a woman being done to

When I went hunting squirrels I felt

The low sound

When the glass jug shuddered

In the earth

*

        We were trapped by the island

        In the middle of the store

        We stood side-by-side but only the rifle

        Could touch us both

        Then the sound, oh… just a low sound

*

Then I

Stepped

Around the island

A Small, Private War

One side

Was heavily

Armored;

The other

Side wore

A soft

Body

And ended

Its days

On the

Grass,

Beside

The dark

Footpath.

from Elements

Deborah Poe

Iron (Fe)

26

an anchor is made not of iron
but stars

your mouth, your mouth
blood poems you moved slowly in me

a hungry body starved

the never today for mañana

more.

Carbon (C)

Spectral
The first picture of earth, you know,
was the one from the spaceship
with the bright yellow gun behind it
lighting up some fine angles
                     for the ever us after.

Roger Revelle knew then
diatoms are sea creatures
the size of a pin head.

And the Dead Sea—between
what is now Israel and Jordan—
was called Lake Asphaltites.

Form
amorphous, powder, and diamond
bucky tubes, wire, and sheet.

graphite, like children, is softest
where diamonds are unyielding.

microscopic diamonds and meteorites.
South African volcanic "pipes."
diamonds recovered from ocean floor
off Senegal's Cape of Good Hope.

how much work is put into understanding
diamonds.

Detemporalized
astroturfing reveals: the earth is so big
we can't have a lasting impact.

watch the carbon dioxide rise
like an aggravated rapist—
temperatures off the chart.

fishing fleets lay impotent teething
on rusted hulks in sand.

Chaba, Songda, Meari, Ma-On, Tokage, Tingting.

(Self)absorption: the moral, ethical imperative.

Retemporalized
Imagine an image of earth—aspiring
in blues and greens.

Oxygen (O)

migrations of distinction

      flower smoke rooms and nail studs

      beat the dog

bridge

      jumping the old bug
      closing the room

  simple-minded patrons
    those simple-minded patrons
     rotten teeth and mussed miss hair

(paint the calendar
girl

      make her clear

      no. make her
      muddy)

irritation of young beard
an old beard last night
   let her be

   let her be
your drunken sailor

bodhisattva's bed
loquats and sticky rice
dumplings for a dragon float

festival in wind and dust
turning the idea

turn her over

smoke wind
behind licking
softly underneath
whispering don't

the grandmother hat
and her buggy child
today on Fox Street bridge

cry distinctly for
the brook underneath

and the girl still
like that forest

says nothing

& the wind
won't weep

Inspired by Gail Hershatter's *Dangerous Pleasures: Prostitution and Modernity in Twentieth-Century Shanghai.*

Flourine (F)

9

this is for you for whom bloom certainly roses...   and all of those doors floating open who have roses going to
those who have roses,   in chambers which those without roses possess no license to enter

skyhook balloon flights detected you   measured   your   relative
abundance
            your cosmic radiation   established the distribution of a nuclear species
      as you stumbled into the atmosphere   albedo and libido spoke in rations
            girls music to remember   eucalyptus and spearmint cool and tender

magnetic fields as if generated by the sun blocked   and led to less reflection

my tongue, my tongue, not your body, my body, my body,   *not yours, while murmuring*
you, while continually murmuring.   you, you, you, which was translated to I no mattter how murmured to whom

readily gaining another   *up a column up to the roof*   I no lighter inert gas

it seems we couldn't place anything beside you in your stream   a spontaneous burst into flame
your diatomic molecules presented in all   states of aggregation—crystal liquid gas

wood and rubber weren't the only things   to burst into flame when held in your stream
            even asbestos reacted vigorously, became incandescent.

as with copper as container   *fox-teeth in your heart*   you coated me

a box of questions shaken up and scattered on the floor, a foot on the stairs, a voice on a wire, a busy collection of
thumbs that imitate fingers, an enemy of yours.   *your lover*

reactive bonded so strongly   so violently I didn't expect you to let go   but great distances
      tinged with distance   *always blue*   *shadows of you named a price*

i dreamed the ocean was very dark. large waves nearly took the diatomic elements   more than once.

Italicized portions of "Flourine" are from Tennessee William's *Androgyne Mon Amour*
(Robert Black's performance).

Boron (B), or Splinter

₅

when you run over the river from school,
you are the height of tall branches

(splinter that. agree on nothing).

      those elegant conjectures,
          whalebone and corset
      a stable covalent bond

*

listen
the poem enjoys the sparrow

further
our windows
are sprung.

*

there is much to do here
in the open backyard
a desire to rip
rip grass
up from its roots
not for weeding
but Destruction

      and spanos
          man, you are the height of tall branches
      you make a decision sound

you, woman, a run-on from the river of school

(fragment. agree on nothing).

the day you fell in love with the wren

breathlessly, the poly-aspirant perspective(s)
weighted
the scope of wind gust retreat.

Italicized portions of "Boron (B), or Splinter" are from Soham Patel's "study the scope of wind gust retreat."

Manganese (Mn)

25

this is not the chemistry of hibiscus blossoms
or the color of lithium steam coming off spring
it is not the Hangzhou rain shower
as tea leaves settle for the day,
or the steady stream of canoe paddling

these shivery nodules, like ancestors,
are immortalized—i mean in ways
loneliness is related to time

abyssal plain still as bodies
bulbous sediment in seabed
unaware this is blackberries' season
with tang off september vine

a moray eel slithers by and by
like rattlesnake looking for sun—
finds only the taste of saltwater
gulps like the taste of skin

the manganese nodules keep growing
centimeters over millions of years—
microbes precipitate hydroxides
seawater breaks down basaltic debris
manganese remobilizes in columns
volcanoes, metals, and springs.

Silver (Ag)

theatre threaten
the knife grief woman
who led tradition astray

beside adam and eve
silver had its genesis beside
the red apple also biblically
introduced with the downfall of man

slag dumps in Asia Minor
and on islands in the Aegean
indicate man learned to separate things

in this case silver from lead
as early as 3000 B.C.

____

pure silver has the highest electrical
and thermal conductivity of all metals,
and possesses the lowest contact resistance.

Mercury (Hg)

80
hydrargyrum meaning watery or liquid silver. a heavy, silvery transition metal, an element liquid near standard room temperature. a noble metal, a heavy metal.

1889
Sun high overhead before leaving the shrine. They too would hire a boat to skirt the Kyushu Western coast, Japan's southernmost island. We are a city located in Kumamoto prefecture.

1908
Nippon Carbide, later Chisso, a company on the shore. Sogi Electric's electric power surged at dusk and dawn. Nippon's name carved along rock and wood.

1932
Graves of cryptomeria everywhere. One large operation, always maintained, pinned to a village made city.

1941
Organic compounds like two halls, one important, one dangerous. Lethal pollutant hammers and blows in rivers and lakes. Industrial wastes settle to river, lake bottoms.

1950
Fishing boats pull together. Children dive for treasures before lightning is caused by something other than heat. A blind singer plays a lute.

1956
An influx of patients—a thousand fish washing to shore.

1965
Patients poisoned from an unknown source scatter downstream along Agano River and coastal regions.

1968
The government's official report on Chisso Minamata's facilities. We follow a road,
stop to see the cave at the edge of Kumamoto.

Two small children dance along behind us. Kasane chants [CH_3Hg].

1969
In fields I watch numbness in the hands and feet, muscle weakness, narrowing
vision, damage to hearing and speech. Insanity, paralysis, coma, death.

Yoko and her foetus in the womb.

Two small children still dance behind.

1972
Venera landed on Venus rather than Mercury. W. Eugene Smith took Tomoko
Uemura's Hand.

1988
Hands busy peeling cucumber and eggplant (Bashō). Some are sentenced guilty. Old
illnesses return, feverish and weak.

1999
Our 1,000 attend Minamata's Disease Victims Memorial. That night it is difficult to
dream.

2006
Forbidden to speak, we are quiet also alone. Knowing mercury's ubiquitous thrust.
Spewing from volcanoes, evaporating off bodies of water, and rising as gas from the
Earth's crust, the poisonous element floats in the air as vapor, binds to particles.

2013
After several days, there will always be clouds gathering over some road. There will
always be a butterfly. And countries far away, until.

from **voyage**

a.rawlings / françois luong

1.

all   shapes   and   names   are   to   be   lost
the further the burrowing goes

not epithelium   the crust
despite its differentiated layers   *veins*
of calcite, sandstone, sulfur   lacks a basal
lamina to support it   growing as
sedimentary layers   lines break into
tectonic incidents   *scars, aquifers, cysts,*
pits   colliding into rifts faults
continents

2.

a   worm   or   a   swarm   of   eyes
festinate   mouths its way through
the ages   *cenozoic, phanerozoic,*
precambrian   leaving a trail
carbon, gelatin, musk, shellac   in
colloidal suspension   not as a way to
escape   as an   urge   to   describe
what is devoured and will surface for
further cataloging

3.

mineral   the mouth closes itself
        slabs of obsidian   obstruction

to the corridor toward the atrium
            the mound   first chamber

of the viscera below   volcanic
strata should fold   hence fractures

and tension lines   a crawl
thru cities of stalactites and

mitral columns   destined
for the core   the surface resists

the drill's assault until a vein
is breached
                     is   opened

4.

      the things that were once lost
being unearthed   even those not
known to be lost   *the first hypotenuse,*
higgs-boson clusters, the final archeography

all sail   freely over an alkaline sea
        shift   under telluric currents
   empty of colors and form in the dark

      a whale's mouth, cauterized

5.

enil a   tolp a strahc
     tsolnu eht fo gniman eht slowly
it   naidisbo fo naeco na moves slowly
mouth unvoiced alveolar trills slowing

drr-drr-drr drr drr the rock hammer

5.

slowly   it moves slowly
it moves   the speed
        a diamond   rill

    mouthing the ashen landscape
with carbon teeth

                revived, the rock
                    the underdark

    hakluyt-by-the-stalagmite   (45°25'17";23°84';-5,698m)
    uqbar the subterranean lake   (46°20';23°87'29";-5,710m)
    merqaba the rift cleaving

        an ocean of obsidian

naming of the unlost
        charts a plot   a line

3.

fold   through cities of stalagmites
grip   lines taut

mineral   mitral
is opened is opening

until a vein   volcanic
is drilled

and tension the mound the corridor
fractures

strata should fold   strata
should fold

6.

A) reduce strength
A) inhibit light transmission
A) split a long a plane a surface a
rhombohedral cubic diagonal
lateral dodecahedral prismatic

Q) is basal slippery
Q) is a body of rock solid
Q) is the separation of a body into
two pieces caused by stress

7.

is the split   of a mass   into mirror images   caused by force
is the partition   of an essence   into twins   caused by emphasis
is the divorce   of the lion's share   into clones   caused by pressure
is the separation   of a body   into two pieces   caused by stress

8.

not fault   nor content   not
drr   drr-drr-drr   drr   drr
riffs   nor incidentally lines
breakage due to lack of
support lost a banal line of
drr drr drr-drr drr-drr drr-drr
despite its differentiated layer
the crust   shifts

I was here   was she
can't remember what letter

A Sequence for Cinematic History

Michael Slosek

Some Pictures Before Here

Returned

the lake is not
what we see.

Erased in the brain
with bird-like decay.

Some of our eyes are taken

Some of the photographic space
in sequence.

The line is back to a wave

and clean—the clear design,
where once too many

Where particles rebound.

Sequence One

After the particles hit
you hear a whistle
as the images cohere.

.

direct in opposition
having lost—

The camera conceals

Parting steel.
Over gate.

.

Several halts

.

Pornographed stone

.

Back in place—write
"the wall out of his mouth."

Hands pass over,
so light and well.

.

They begin to have their story here.
A necessary vessel pushes from the shadows
in removable years.

Sequence One

elements have
what we think of

simple reduction,
pieced upon.

.

Dense—
what night gets doubled
in symmetry

.

He stands, but if speaking
would crumble

.

"to dream of speed
where the *d*
gets minor"

.

The house then:

Not where the glass is missing
or where they have kept the shovel.

.

In buildings once part
of a great white fire.

Sequence Two

For a field and a car
following where we discard
the dissonant mark—

"did he say was there"
And the point of the question was
to ask how far.

.

Swallowing hard.
The grossly over-painted lake
shelling their ice to trial.

.

In a film
the mapped static shows a highway
of continuous proportion

where air intrudes.

.

He is driving and speaking
of a lost door—and the denial of stone

somewhere before
first staged flowerbomb.

Three Versions of the Imaginary

Spun, where a head is grown
backwards, to its root.
Inside the reversal of blood
where the first line rhymes with the last one.

So what might be
the loss of language
or simple forgetting
(where "so" and "or" are interchanged)

calling to each other
becomes a form of silence, shifting
in the sentence, down
to an accidental darkness.

Sequence Five

In the first mode
we watch the composition of a square.

Each wanting to double,
made of snow and spare parts.

"Did you see his dream
protracted through disaster"

Done, the exact damage
running out of ink.

.

Underneath adding—
a system of squares
passively holds.

The rhythm destructs the sequence—
known in relation to alone.

The sets are composed of
and exclude each other.

We've said this before.

.

Inside the signs are dying

or underneath, value added
through a hole of ink.

The autobiotic lifts his weight

tho the east is the darkest point.

The figure decomposes over a bridge.

Sequence Six

Contained in a book that spirals apart.
This luck, and photographed his face.

8

The road is given of decomposed moths.
The body of a dog and shadow of a bat.

8

Recombinatory patterns, squares in a cell,
the cell aligned with nervatic wiring.

8

Subtone in a minor substance, as *a*
unwound in the note's underground.

8

Today, rust of a gun. Shadow
of a beard, smoke in the blood.

8

The bomb is based in pearl, the walls
embossed in the symbolist's yellow.

8

A story, two lines apart, a
place registered in sun——the onyx sea.

8

Fleece at the end of air, teeth of a cage,
alphabet inside an open afterdoor.

8

As an ink faded border guard,
and those years, the world retards.

8

No one gets up, ash alights the stair,
proceeds from familiar patterns.

8

To complete, the open syn
aptic relation to salt, to wind.

8

An alibi will substitute language
for speaking, a cell, and the soloist's string.

Sequence Seven

Mostly not,
unfinished
in a cryotext.

We couldn't walk
through transparent albums
and model guns,

as white as the eyes
in black and white
photostock
ground to a halt.

The underground
where leaf-joints solder
their arms,

a meal of noise
chemical limbs
and body of tongue.

Sequence Fragment

There the note that given
climbed a hole in space

and turned, endlessly ringing—
Until their syllogism in skin
walked backward to sleep.

from **SPECIAL MANAGE MEET**

Kevin Thurston

MANAGE HOURS

Because the required (daily)
    is constantly changing
(a daily   & an A:M − P:M basis)
        continuously manage both
pro-actively & re-actively.

The managing of hours is absolutely mandatory
to achieve productivity gains & is the top
3 important responsibilities.

All will not experience the same
(labor) requirements in the same way or at
the same time.

        OTHER FACTORS
Yes people are punched but are they
producing (productive)   .
continuously moniter & correct

- Wandering
- Spending time
- Discussions

- Excessive "trips" to "solve problems"
- Wasting time
- Disappeering

COORDINATION

Cannot be created

    & the timing of
work & output

EXAMPLES
- Hours
- Hours
- Times
- Times
- Rush
- Time effects

INPUT & OUTPUT
    mandatory that
(take into) consideration.   Needs &
requirements of the other.

    Answering is useless unless
created.

    Voicing is the final step & is always
necessary & creates the makes.

WAGE PROGRAM

Almost everyone who starts   has a 3
month period with   increases at
the end of   satisfactory progress.

        After that,   depends on individual
        performance & performance.

        Measure this performance &
                    called productivity.

        Low or non existant productivity:
                low or non existant   increases

        A given that everyone has
        to be productive

        in other words   to develope
                        improve
        output (for a given amount of time)

        Unproductive   or individual
                    not increase
        output (for a given period of time)

        Productive   or individual
                    does increase
        output (for a given period of time)

        In a competitive   &
                measuring
            place.   the
        results   from someone else

In a competitive   &
            measuring
    order.   the
results   from someone else

We cannot, just,
            unproductive
        increase yours &
    be productive &
increase in   will allow   to
proportionatly distribute

BOTTOM LINE

MANAGE SKILLS

Of being, a manage at   it
     to come more complex & consume
          an increases in skills & skill

Being doesn't mean a title and
wearing a name.

     "MANAGE"
Means, a group (of people)
For   every aspect
  a team dedicated to,
to   expectations.

     "MANAGE"   part of manage &
Means,   therefore
responsible.   A designated portion.
                    & duties.
leads, controls, executes &
that is expected.

     "MANAGE"
Means?
Many books have been written to help & advise,
manage.   vast majority of,
by, professors or academics or others   (little or)
no actual. "Manage" experience. Being
is   tough   .   Means, constantly (balancing)
between
                    &
sometimes chaotic atmosphere.

CONTROLLED REQUIREMENTS

EXAMPLES OF   CAN'T CONTROL

-
-
-
-
-
-

EXAMPLES OF   CAN CONTROL

-
-
-
-
-
-

COST OF TALKING

Engage in
Ingage is non
conversation cost—
it reduces
        ability

            INDIRECT
Constant talking
while pretending. Regardless
of what
within listening range &
it directed to has.
                    It sets
a very unimpressive
control, attitude & responsibility.
Increase is reduced by this
type of behavior.

            DIRECT
Same as above but with no pretense

            TELEPHONE
Personal   , inbound or outbound
                increase anxiety &
        disrupt .

            INTER
                or actual conversations
Intercom calls between dept personell that have no
        purpose or a non-urgent purpose are
non productive

            INTRA
Same as above but within

COST
         every minute represents
10¢.
    . When this occurs

                                 a

phantom   is getting paid

COST OF WALKING

A physically large building (broken
up)   . When
        without stopping it takes 4 minutes.
Is it a productive "walk" or is just an excuse?

        TYPES OF WALKING
                • WANDERING •
                usually   carrying
                & an urgent facial appearance
                to convince others
                a useful official purpose
                • INTER •
                same as above but twice as unproductive.
                • INTRA •
                same as above
                • OUTSIDE THE BUILDING OR IN THE
                        ROOM •
                anyone who in the room
                or outside the building
                                is in violation of
                                & is subject to dismissal.
                Exceptions could include trash,
                        or the very short time
                microwave heating of food or drink.
                • PRODUCTIVITY •
All activities reduce productivity &
reduce their own (&) ability s.

MANAGE MUST MANAGE

Manage
    manage team & run
productive   maintaining
    , moral & output.

    THIS INVOLVES BUT IS NOT LIMITED
        TO THE FOLLOWING

- Visual
- Verbal
- Actions
- In-actions
- Company
- Responsibility
- Accountability

- Personal
- Prejudice
- Favoritism
- Fairness
- Attitude
- Setting example
-

When possible,   practice to
appoint   from
population. The transition
        is difficult. It creates stress.
It can create jealousy. It can breed resentment.
It requires doing "now" things, some easy, some
difficult.

Responsibility &   accountability. A
, in the eyes of most   , is
        Manage says, does, acts &
looks determines
                worth

All are not created equal &
                    . But all
manage, must manage. Proactive
not reactive.   Solve   not create
                    responsible for
          an efficient productive.

PROBLEMS

we have 10
     common problems
and unique problems.
   All   have problems.
   Manage
Responsibility proactively &
reactively promptly & consistently
locate   .
   You active
manage   the designated
to accomplish.
Grows, its
must also grow.   showing up
in a blue sweater & sitting
     does not mean you
      manage.
To continue, manage,
  require a productive,
efficient & accurate   .
Means manage people. Its not easy.
Relationships always
a fine line.
     Gaining
without compromising   is
a never ending task.

The sunset is a 'Flowing identity rutabaga' etc.

Hannah Rodabaugh

The sunset is a 'Flowing identity rutabaga'

"The perpetuity of matter is our prime motivator: truth is many colors."

1

The purpose of mind is to clot thought.

A Flub *or*
Fib tab
Ow end,
Rub bag(*s*)
Low indent,
A Rut din wing:
Rust loft , Id,
Idit, 'idée fi(*x*)' : tabla *tabula*.
Win grids of rye,
A table tang, a frag diet
Deirt; fort ray in
Forty day(*s.*)

2

Metonymy

Ratta tatta ratta tatta
Whooooooooo-oooooo
Doncha cold cream that bunting orange
Doncha whimple on that egg *ooooohhh*
Whig sag clover caught in guilt
Ad soft steam dozers or lowering silt
Cream saddle Un sided itself
Caught in birds of furr
That whistle the clouds until they scram
Ble over usping birch seated
Sea Of
Red and red and red
The sard or cling into the hold
Hat sting,
Sowing Pig pink
You meta stink

3

A more 'concrete' example.

'Layer one'
P-rple purple purrle
Rubflinf purkle blugit prrp blue and blister butter redug pin king
Whit whi-tea whi-tearing wha wha whet
Yaller holler yella that cling ding fella slow in the b sang-gah
Yal yalderoll stippa stippa gunt gold groove mister ding
Whig, toreador of what(e) whaite why-ete unt uncka untint tart
Plural-sa husserl transcribbit pinkart pinksling shower us wif clea n
Pink pink pink start unto unit or=wh witr pin pinsky pinsky stunt.   I want

This fall of clover
soft
Like rockes Agate
Read.

Teach to tattle on others
Books are a brown nosers
Handshake
What you want to bake inside your brain pan
Is fake

Take
From your pan
The pan that reeds
Of
Fuggit
Foget
Fudgeut

To unstow
It to know less
Than what you are
Fidgeting to
Express

anja: the winged perceiver

beyond what
this is

you fall
in stars
of
wet color
two petals
of perfect
arboreal blue

we waste from
vision/vice
cistern/unprepossessing
what/toothsoflight
stay/succor
offist/grist
gold/oiled
into/aspring
caught
up
in
thrombosis

westgetsyou
anywhere
anywhere

Pinchent penchants/Oinchant oenchants (An Aubade)

Ointchants
Chants
Chant Gigigigigigigive
RrrrrrestHomeless
In yourn breast
Ho slowly you
Blued like
Ytaod Inroad

Graves Of sacked
Hot andb Ahsed Gonna see the sun Commin cmiin

Deare
Sjdhcjcjcsdklajlakdjvcdvjdn   heroditussssss
Dnvlajvlah   Deeliylahs
Sfblzjvlsjvnl; force
Scbjdsbc   was cleanin
Mvcbfvuhjv   into the (h)air
Bcjhcof watery dawn
Sfngfj the sun
Still has his long rubbed suede
Hammered dulcimer
In chords
redDreams a little
bittle dirp drunk
clouds clunk
The skyInto
One big jamboree
Pie Of nautilus
Ices stork
Lenticlar
Fences of bolshy cream

Shod with nuggets
 Of shingle
Warped
Sour-up
Lumps of
Gold   Trousers
With s(t)eams
Of exetrons
Prismatic suspension
divine
In vertebrate

Red petals
Sort me
I was watching the tulip abstract
My nature

From its yawning mo( )th
Teeth roan of
Long

Lawn of ilean
On
Loted
Stro

Crismpo
Jiker

Gi

THE A DOWN

Tawrin Baker

"would go great with"

The master list of immortal forces. "Carla honey where'd we eat last week" she
would of seen if she knew the words for it. Especially how we "take me, Brian!"
use them that she don't know, full up of judgment and terror she can't imagine.
That's hell in this world, what we put in a person.

**Determined his default logic's
Struggling within a sick metaphysic.**

"What I mean is when I think maybe I identify with certain thoughts, maybe
that's——and they might jump from this to that, and all the while I'm scratching my
ass, shifting in my chair. Someone might come over and say 'hi' absentmindedly
and my attention's on them, but it's still not me who's acting there, the center" I
know that that's a tree "held barely edges in——*the worn curtains revealing of an ecology
of social surplus, as fruit color energetic surplus*——holding"

Have we the power, now, to bend down the world of myth, the living artifice, and bind it to our science?

Baloney. Sister Mary Margaret said "kerplunk." battles " 'Sup?" tamber "the thingk machine amazing grace a" ba ba ba blew it! "Tink, tink!" fucker face "Did you tell on her" pbbttttt! "brother?" Bother?

We're in a hard prison, we can barely move.

Did you hear? Last "flooded dendrites—I think a serotonin overabundance resulting from" consulting firm's legal liability very cleverly minimized by "overloaded with groceries" I wish—I wish! that this "the last 2006 state construction budget" make a wonderful addition to your home or office "would be a fairy princess. I would flit in the magical air between" because 'would' is death

It is a terror that only the imagination is real.

I don't remember much but let me try. Halos around the lamplights in the mugginess and I took note of how the neighbors set up their porches all empty of people. The night thick. Got a Mountain Dew from the gas station because of a headache, not sure what I was thinking about. Smoked a cigarette, stepped around some mud so it wouldn't stick to my sandals. The weeds and well tended bushes. Kids from the bars in an SUV drove by, one of them shaking a tambourine sort of singing out the window. I flicked the butt to the street but only made it to the edge of grass. Turned the corner home, walked quietly. Nothing touched me I'm an adult.

That Hispania couldn't maintain her technology was surely a sign of poverty.

Come down, come down "your mom told me tell you you" can you feel it tonight, Alexander? It's a night, I'm sure, that will change all of history—you'll "memory. Memory—my pussy

When the levee breaks

hurts too." to give my home a shove "*nailed* him against the boards drawing a"You'd think I'd had enough of him, and I have. You tell me and I know, he's no good. But it's like eating, it's not always necessity. Sometimes—and everyone if only for minutes has—you fatten yourself. I believe there's a simplicity in resignation, and if it's a worn, tired beauty, still you can be convinced it's true beauty; that the greatest love is surrender; is endurance.

Bureaucratic order forms.

I've made a few assumptions, but have yet to work out their conclusions. For instance, take "the first principle," that of non-contradiction. "For instance. Take" the first principle "that of non-contradiction," take the first "that" of the "non-contradiction" principle for "of for the" that instance principle, take first "non-contradiction."

"I was born in those awkward teenage years, and in them I will die."

The first instance. Then a second mistake. Break another dish and we're dropping you. "tear you apart and see what sick contradictions within" would imply what about non-contradiction? "Be a—ably state—inhere in. Reside." I'm telling you she's a type. Phony, manipulative, sucking the attention of every man in the room. I'd be happy if she died.

The tongue tends its own intelligence
Hidden from you in darkness.

Take a fucking stand. "And slap it on a bumper sticker. Make it fucking catchy. Sellable positions your enemies will envy" ten of these please—please? "Go. Distort the courts. I had an abortion." For the past twenty years I've been working on surrender. I've been working for a split second some fragment of this vast array of *perceptible*. "If I were to put it in those terms it's like the ego is another's—an appendage, flapping. More, something like—then alone again, reading" like the swerve, you know? Thanks. As a crude analogy, take this constant mass of mechanical causation as a falling, these particles of 'what', straight down. An utterly complex sequence yet, lacking will, atemporal. Then something deep, an urge which is like grace bubbles up from an infinite distance and wham! out goes a kick from my now charged body, a stray jerk recoiling my hips, my shin hits hard on the coffee table—and it's not triumphant, or absurd, it didn't even happen. The action's been absorbed, explained away,

Monopole.

and the bruised fucking shin's no memory. "I forgot how good he looks." in
becoming sensitive again. "Tell me your name again, I forget so quickly" don't—
stop and remember where was put "thank you for" for—

"to modulate the heart's mouth"

"for what? To make and make over is" tonight I'll not——the wind to leaves'
sound——his hands not young but yet pristine, potential——fumbling "saw a great
movie yesterday" Oh did you? Oh! "I'm talking about technology here." To whom?
I thought you made arrangements already. Look, call yourself, he has a place
because he called himself, and I can't guarantee there will be any room left.

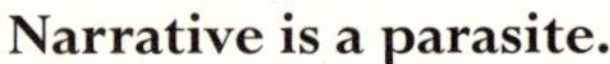

Narrative is a parasite.

And you should do it today.

Living communication—which is being—is

on surrender to G-d. "And then he" (oh) "—'d me, and it felt like a kiss." *Here, then.* "If you were Maxwell's Demon and I didn't pass your test—would you still let me in? What would it cost you, baby? How much would you spend?" telling you I think the solution is love and compassion. *A quick assembly.* Now, they are not taught, they're willed, they come from within—hold, just wait. Empathy is God made flesh, and words are a world of agent intellects. We wrestle with them as with Angels " 'tween our two psychologies a desolate plain where 'tween"

Lost, unfelt, to its black mouth.

. . (even such simple acts—are impossible to insist, impossible to project with confident prediction from our conception of outw— " I promise you, now—that this love won't be forever. You are more beautiful, even, than all I haven't seen. That you will always be so desirable; that you will wrest, with your barest gesture, new love from a succession of myselves; that you

Combanatrix.

—impossibly prior— , " ':;.,) "

an—an an of the—it by the, it it by and above the and—by above, above, above of
of the, of of and the, of it of it

the of of the of the—by an above it, and it an and and an an and—the it of it above
an of of it—and the above above it it of and and the

it it and by an above it of

Brokeback!

Loudly, "Where Teesha at? Where Teesha at?" (Pause) Tenderly, "*Put her on.*"
(Pause) Loudly, "You do like I told you? You do like I told you?"
(Pause) Tenderly, "*Okay. Yeah.*" (END CALL)

Art is my god, I'll have no other.

"Then: that this situation is all the other sicknesses past. That, when it gets
bad, there is an identical desire to skip it all until mended, and that this eternal,
recurring wish, after a mostly forgotten agony, has always been, always is, granted.
But if sick I'm so in the present, suffering from being bound to future agony. The
'I' is that this *now* will pass, too, to a vague memory, an idea of"

Bounce that ass

snow now enormous in the streetlights "shadows rose to the buildingtops and after"
on a clear night away from light pollution "is a steam radiator, right?" mythic—
present—sight shining out the stars "outside with closed eyes in any weather" when,
the first spring night warm enough to crack open windows, wind in—

I just wanna work that surface.

Look at him now! Imagine him, upset as he drives to pick up his daughter, crashing
into—there's a lot on his mind, after all! "Which way did you" where do the days
go, oh where's the time go "and after all this you expect me" THERE IS NO SUCH
THING AS NARRATIVE THAT REALLY "Ugh, I can't stand your chatter! If I
could break up with you and be alone to think—you are such an obligation! Why
isn't it allowed that I upset you? I can upset myself any time I want, and that for the
good!"

We loved with a love that was love than love—

at times a thought breaks, not even such a mass of habits "but really, I think we all—maybe if it comes to that—and" 2375 net weight; 4 door / did she "luminous, fell past the black brink, shining all" screw him. And fuck you too "Nowhere is it said that 'aliquid quod nihil maius cogitari possit' isn't" but the whole idea's wrong, because

Partly because I like to keep it fresh, and avoid adapting, and partly because my schedule is subject to interruptions and I need to workout when I can, however I can.

Since our hip flexors are generally stronger than our ab muscles, we rely on them by yanking ourselves up as our hip flexors tug on our spine. But she was also able to talk and laugh as we visited and I told her I was proud of her for that, and for so many things. The former you can get from watching. The circumstances that led to the victim going to the floor included noise, terror, seeing others shot, concern for his classmate, overwhelming confusion about what to do. But laying on the floor is a bad idea. But laying on the floor is a bad idea. CCC Here at World Stock Report we work on what we here from the street. Big news expected. This should invoke LARGE gains.

This is another source of lower back strain. And if you like sparring, then do that. I change my routine all the time. Or run for the door and figure we may get shot in the back or legs or whatever. The latter only comes by doing. Basically, you do a bridge with your head off the floor, then lift each arm and leg in succession. And if you like sparring, then do that. I workout before workouts. Try his tips below and get an instant boost to your martial arts. The next step is to run circles around the bat. The former you can get from watching. And when we get to the stressful parts, and the scary parts if we can keep our sense of humor that shows maturity. Eventually, it worked. We did the baseball bat drill in Kung Fu class the other night and it was hilarious—I mean highly instructive! It will also keep you aware of levels at which you may be over doing it if you experience muscle, tendon, or joint soreness. My flinching stopped. Keeping a journal will help track progress. I intended to reprint it here, but my email application crashed and I lost it. Enthusiasm revives us. You can do this either standing up, or in the bent over row position. Try his tips below and get an instant boost to your martial arts. Stay safe, come home soon. Do a set of reps with the palms down, and then a set with the palms up. Now, touch your forehead to the top of the bat. After that, I recommend people try to cut their time. I workout before workouts. Enthusiasm revives us. The result is that my training can begin sliding sideways instead of forward. Then one wintry day here in beautiful Washington, D. Simply measure your waist at the belly button, and your hips at the buttoxx, then divide waist by hips. As the door flew open one of her classmates yelled for her to get under a desk. Or run for the door and figure we may get shot in the back or legs or whatever. Your back should be rounded. The next step is to run circles around the bat. Try his tips below and get an instant boost to your martial arts. Try his tips below and get an instant boost to your martial arts. My flinching stopped. The main thing is to give your hands a workout. I change my routine all the time. You want to step into the ring with some snap still in your muscles.

Kate Schapira—see: *Phoenix Memory* (horse less press, 2007), *The Saint's Notebook* (CAB/NET Chapbook Series, 2007)—see also: *Aufgabe, blazeVOX, word for/word, Coconut, Denver Quarterly, Cordite*—curator of Providence-based reading series *Publicly Complex* (www.ada-books.com)—**Barrett Gordon**—see: *rainbow-grey* (House Press, 2006), *graverubber* (House Press, 2006), *Of a Free Town* (w/ Luke Daly, House Press, 2005)—see also: *Drill, Small Town*—co-editor of *string of small machines* (w/ Luke Daly and Eric Unger)—member of House Press (www.housepress.org)—**Jennifer Karmin**—see: *Myth of Me* (Ragamuffin Press, 1996)—see also: *Bird Dog, MoonLit, Disaster, Blue Beat Jacket, Milk Magazine, Seven Corners, WOMB*—see also: *The City Visible: Chicago Poetry for the New Century* (Cracked Slab Books, 2007)—co-curator of the Chicago-based Red Rover Series (www.groups.yahoo.com/group/redroverseries)—currently: instructor at Truman College and Poet-in-Residence for the Chicago Public Schools—**Stephanie Strickland**—see: *V: WaveSonnets/Losing L'una* (Penguin Books, 2002), *True North* (University of Notre Dame Press, 1997), *The Red Virgin: A Poem of Simone Weil* (University of Wisconsin Press, 1993), *Give the Body Back* (University of Missouri Press, 1991)—digital poetry: *slippingglimpse* w/ Cynthia Lawson Jaramillo and Paul Ryan (www.slippingglimpse.org), *V:Vniverse* w/ Cynthia Lawson (www.vniverse.com)—co-editor of *Electronic Literature Collection, volume 1* (www.collection.eliterature.org/1)—forthcoming: *Zone: Zero* (Ahsahta Press, 2008)—**Mathew Timmons**—see: *Manufactured Inspiration, Greetings, Disaster, Sleepingfish, P-Queue, Holy Beep!, Kadar Koli*—co-editor of Insert Press (w/ Stan Apps)—co-host and co-producer of internet radio show *LA-Lit* (w/ Stephanie Rioux)—co-curator of *Late Night Snack* literary cabaret (w/ Harold Abramowitz)—currently: program coordinator of CalArts MFA Writing Program, teaches at CalArts School of Critical Studies—forthcoming: *a particular vocabulary* (w/ Marcus Civin, P S Books: The Particle Series)—online: (www.anathematas.blogspot.com)—**Kaethe Schwehn**—see: *Crazyhorse, jubilat, Forklift, Ohio, The Literary Review, Faultline, The Cresset, Open Letters*—see also: book reviews at *CutBank* (www.cutbankpoetry.blogspot.com)—currently: visiting assistant professor at St. Olaf College—acknowledgement: "Me to Tanka" originally published in *Crazyhorse*—**Jaye Bartell**—forthcoming: *Acres of Ourselves* (House Press, 2008), *Coasts* (Red Hen Press, 2008)—see: *CutBank, Rivendell, Capgun*—**Jessica Smith**—see: *Organic Furniture Cellar* (Outside Voices, 2006)—editor of *FOURSQUARE* (www.foursquare editions.blogspot.com)—member of House Press (www.housepress.org)—online: (www.looktouch.blogspot.com)—**David Pavelich**—see: *Ash* (Bronze Skull Press, 2004), *Outlining* (Cuneiform Press, 2003)—see also: *Antennae, Aufgabe, Bird Dog, LVNG, Chattahoochee Review, Crayon, The Progressive Librarian*—editor of Answer Tag chapbooks and broadsides (www.answertaghomepress.com)—currently: special collections librarian and bibliographer for contemporary and modern poetry at the University of Chicago—**Erin M. Bertram**—see: *Alluvium* (dancing girl press, 2007), *Here, Hunger* (w/ Sarah Lilius, NeO Pepper Press, 2007)—see also: *Bloom, The Laurel Review, Best New Poets 2007*—forthcoming: *Body Of Water* (Thorngate Road)—editor of shadowbox press (www.shadowboxpress.blogspot.com)—currently: fellow/instructor in the MFA Writing Program at Washington University in St. Louis—acknowledgement: "[My Tattoo]" originally published in *CutBank,* "[Leaning On The Limits Of Myself]" originally published in *Knockout*—**Laura Sims**—see: *Practice, Restraint* (Fence Books, 2005)—see also: *Paperback Book* (3rd Bed, 2006), *Bank Book* (Answer Tag Press, 2004)—see also: *CAB/NET, Crayon, First Intensity, 26, How2, 6X6*—forthcoming: *Stranger* (Fence Books, 2008)—**Deborah Poe**—see: *The Sensual Infrastructure* (Stockport Flats, 2006)—see also: *Many Mountains Moving, Copper Nickel, Caesura, Drunken Boat*—see also: *Fingernails Across the Chalkboard: Poetry and Prose on HIV/AIDS From the Black Diaspora*—forthcoming: *Our Parenthetical Ontology* (CustomWords, Fall 2008)—online: (www.deborahpoe.com)—acknowledgement: "Boron, or Splinter" originally published in *Denver Quarterly*—**a.rawlings**—see: *Wide slumber for lepidopterists* (Coach House Books, 2006), *W I D E R* (Belladonna Books, 2006)—editor of *Shift & Switch: New Canadian Poetry* (Mercury Press, 2005)—online: (www.commutiny.blogspot.com)—**françois luong**—see: *New American Writing, Hot Whiskey, Switchback, Spell*—co-editor of *blowfish* (www.blowfishjournal.org)—online: (www.fluong.blogspot.com)—**Michael Slosek**—see: *Z Formation* (Katalanche Press 2007), *By the Weight of an Arrow* (w/ Luke Daly, House Press 2007), *Each In Neither* (House Press, 2006)—see also: *Aufgabe, Mirage/Period(ical), Spell, Small Town, Plantarchy*—editor of *Drill* (2002-2006)—member of House Press (www.housepress.org)—curator of the House Press Bay Area Reading Series—currently: works for the University of California Press—**Kevin Thurston**—see: *fHole, yt communications, the new chief tongue, O Outbreak* (Furniture Press, 2005)—forthcoming: chapdisc *KEVIN is running late* (narrowhouse recordings)—curator for Just Buffalo Small Press Poetry Series (www.justbuffalo.org)—co-organizes the Buffalo Small Press Book Fair (www.buffalosmallpress.org)—online: (www.fucking lies.blogspot.com)—**Hannah Rodabaugh**—see: *Ludlow Garage*—listen: OGADE African drum ensemble—currently: MA student in creative writing at Miami University—**Tawrin Baker**—see: *So That Even / A Lover Exists* (House Press, 2007), *Th* (House Press, 2006)—forthcoming: *The Break Down* (House Press)—member of House Press (www.housepress.org)—